THE ISLAND CLANS DURING
SIX CENTURIES

The Island Clans During Six Centuries

By

The Rev. Canon

R.C. MacLeod of MacLeod

AUTHOR OF "THE MACLEODS OF DUNVEGAN,"
AND "THE MACLEODS, THEIR HISTORY
AND TRADITIONS."

SCOTPRESS
Morgantown, West Virginia
1984

First published by Robert Carruthers & Sons
Reprinted 1984 by SCOTPRESS
P.O. Box 778
Morgantown, West Virginia

ISBN 0-912951-13-3

CONTENTS.

CHAPTER I

THE NORSE OCCUPATION OF THE HEBRIDES.

EFFECTS ON THE RACE TO WHICH THE PEOPLE BELONG— THEIR LANGUAGE, THEIR ART, THE LAWS WHICH GOVERNED THE OWNERSHIP OF LAND, AND THE SUCCESSION TO DIGNITIES.

The Norse occupation of the Hebrides and of some of the mainland of Scotland has left much more important and lasting results than is generally realised. If we consider the length of time during which this occupation lasted it would be strange if it had not exerted a great influence in many directions.

The raids of Norse pirates began at a very early period. There may be some doubt as to whether the burning of the religious houses at Eigg in April 617 was the work of Norsemen, but the repeated attacks on Iona between 794 and 825 were certainly carried out by them, and, indeed, all the West Coast of Scotland as far as Galloway in the south was being constantly laid waste by Norse rovers during the first half of the ninth century.

Probably the brochs and duns were built by the Celtic inhabitants during this period as places of defence against the Norse raiders. These are found in large numbers wherever the Vikings are known to have come, and they are found in no other part of Scotland. We may look on them, therefore, as records of the appalling period during which the Western Isles were being ravaged by the Vikings.

These raids, however, destructive as they were, could have no permanent results on the character of the people who suffered from them ; but, towards the end of the ninth century, the Norsemen began to settle in the Western Isles. Harold Haarfagre had made himself Master of all Norway, instigated by the ambitious lady he wished to marry. The numerous petty kings who had ruled as independent sovereigns on the

Fjords of Norway, unable to resist, and unwilling to submit, sailed forth to carve out for themselves new principalities in the west. Some went to England, some to France, some to Italy, some took service in the famed Varangian guard at Constantinople, many found new homes in the Isle of Man and in Ireland, and towards the end of the ninth, and during the tenth century, the Vikings were settling in the Hebrides, reducing the Celtic chiefs to obedience, and making the Islands their own.

They did not exterminate the Celtic inhabitants of the country. It was not to their interest to do so ; their own numbers were not very large, and they needed people to cultivate the soil, to row their dragon ships, and to perform other menial duties. Probably some of the Celtic tribes may still have retained possession of their lands, but it is certain that by the end of the tenth century the Norwegians had become predominant in the Western Isles ; as indeed they were in the Orkneys and Shetlands, in the north-east of Scotland, on the seaboard of Ireland, and in the Saxon kingdom of Northumbria.

The early Norse settlers in the Western Isles were independent chieftains ; they had thrown off the authority of the Norwegian kings, and owed obedience to no one. But their situation made it necessary that they should combine together for purposes of mutual defence, and some union of this sort, under kings of Norse descent, became an accomplished fact at an early period. In the middle of the tenth century, Magnus MacArailt was *rex plurimarum insularum*. His brother Godred was King of Man and the Isles in 979. We find several others mentioned as Kings of the Isles, and in 1066, Godred Crovan founded the dynasty which was destined to rule for 200 years over Man and the Isles.

Meanwhile the King of Norway was taking steps to assert his authority. As early as 890 he sent an army under Ketil Flatneb, who reduced the Norsemen on the mainland to obedience, and 200 years later the expeditions of Magnus Barefoot, the first of which took place in 1092, settled the question of Norwegian supremacy over the kings of Man and the Isles. Whatever they had been before, hence-forth these were tributary kings owning obedience to the King of Norway, and paying him " Scat."

Not only were the islands Norwegian from a political point of view, but they were also Norwegian ecclesiastically. The see of the Syderies and Man (now corrupted to Sodor and Man) was in the province of Throndjhem, and its Bishop was under the control of the Norwegian Archbishop. This state of affairs lasted till 1266, when the Western Isles were ceded to Alexander III., King of Scotland, by Haakon, King of Norway. Thus for more than four hundred years the Western Isles were under Norse rule. So prolonged an occupation was bound to have very important results, and I shall consider these under five heads.

I. I take first the race to which the people of the Islands belong. There can be no doubt that the Norse and the Celtic people of the country freely intermarried. It is probable that Somerled, the famous founder of the great MacDonald family, was of mixed descent. His own name is Norse, as are the names of his sons, Reginald and Olave, and though he may have been a Celt in the male line, he certainly had Norse blood in him. Probably even the clans which appear to be purely Celtic have Norsemen among their ancestors. In spite of Skene's opinion, after carefully sifting all the available evidence, I am convinced that the MacLeods are mainly of Norse descent, though they too probably have Celtic blood in their veins.

As with the chiefs, so with the masses of the people. I am convinced that they are not pure-blooded Celts. The Islesmen of the present day show qualities very different from those of the Celtic races, and those qualities are due to the mixture of Norse blood in them.

Firstly, compared with the Irish, the West Highlanders are a law-abiding people. For many years, owing to the pressure of hard economic facts, they have lived in great poverty. They have believed that they were suffering great injustice, and for a time they had agitators among them who urged them to take the law into their own hands, and right their wrongs by force. In a very few cases they acted on those pernicious counsels.

They drove the stock off land which they desired to occupy as small-holders, and took possession of some farms. But there were no murders of landowners or factors, there was no maiming of cattle, there were no outrages, there was no secret drilling with a view to an armed rising against the Government. Even when the crofter agitation was its height, there was only very little of the lawlessness which was such a deplorable feature of similar crises in Ireland.

Some years ago a remarkable instance of the West Highlander's reverence for law came under my observation. I was told that a number of men proposed to raid a farm in the neighbourhood. I asked them to meet me and talk the matter over, and we had a long and most friendly discussion. In the course of this I used every argument I could think of to dissuade them from their proposed action. Among other things I pointed out that to drive off a man's stock, and seize the land of which he was lawfully possessed, was to rob him of his means of living, and practically amounted to a breach of the Eighth Commandment. They accepted this, and refrained from raiding the land. I do not think it can be denied that on the whole the West Highlanders are a law-abiding people.

Secondly, when they go abroad they make most excellent emigrants. They do not like going, they have the Celtic love of home very strongly developed in them ; they are not an enterprising people, and it cannot be said that they are very strenuous and hard-working at home. Therefore, one would not credit them with possessing qualities likely to make them successful pioneers in a new country. But, when West Highlanders get into one of the Colonies, all their lack of energy disappears as if by magic. They become vigorous workers, they almost invariably do well, and, though from generation to generation they retain their love of their old homes in Skye or the Long Island—in many cases they still speak the language of their fathers—they have become invaluable citizens of the colony in which they live.

In one respect it is strange that the Norse blood in their veins does not appear to have influenced them. The Norse were essentially lovers of the sea. "The hardy Norseman's home of yore was on the foaming wave," and their descendants in Norway itself and on the East Coasts of England and Scotland continue to carry on the old tradition ; but it cannot be said that the Scottish Islanders, though they live on the sea, take kindly to a seafaring career.

II. The language of the Highlanders at first sight seems to be purely Celtic, and, if this were really the case, it might be argued—Gaelic being the language of the people—that no Norse conquest of the country had ever taken place at all. But the Norse influence on the Gaelic language has really been very strong. In his *Norse Influence in Celtic Scotland*, Dr Henderson gives a list of several hundred Gaelic words which are derived from the Norse. Many of the surnames still borne by Highlanders are Norse. MacLeod, MacCaskill, MacIvor, Macaulay, Gunn, Tolmie, McCrailt, are a few instances out of many which might be named. A large number of the Christian names which occur in West Highland history, some of which are still borne by living Highlanders, are Norse names. Tormod, anglicized to Norman, is the Norse Thormodhr, Thor minded ; Torquil is the Norse Thorkill, Thor's kettle ; Godfrey, the Norse Gudrod ; Reginald is the Norse Rognvaldr, Ruler from the Gods ; Ronald is another form of the same name. Somerled is a Norse name meaning " the summer sailor," that is, the Viking who went on ravaging expeditions in summer.

Here again many other instances could be given. But it is in the place-names all over the Islands that the Norse influence has been strongest. In Lewis and Harris three-fourths of the important place-names are Norse, in Skye a very large proportion. All the place-names terminating in bost, nish, and a, ay, or ey are Norse, " bost " meaning a township or stead, " nes " meaning a point or promonotory, " ey " meaning an island. As most Highlanders know, these are very common terminations. Indeed, ninety per cent. of the Islands have names terminating in some form of the Norse " ey." Many other places are known by Norwegian names. Uig is the Norse " Vik," a bay, from which comes the word Viking ; Sleat or Slate in Skye is the Norse " Sletta," a plain ; Staffa and Staffin are both derived from the Norse. Staffa means a staff, or rod, to which their basaltic rocks bear a resemblance.

Uist is the Norse Ivist, a habitation. Eriscay is Eric's island, Barra is Barr's island, Barr being a contraction of St Findbarr, a saint whose day was kept on September 25th. Though Mull has retained its pre-Norse name, half the place-names in the island are of Norse origin. Jura is pure Norse, and means deer's isle.*

Some names which seem to be Gaelic may possibly be really Norwegian. Such a one is Dunvegan. It appears at first sight to be Gaelic, dun bheagan, " the little dun," but it may really be " Bekan's Dun." There is a place in Iceland called Bekansstad, and it is possible that this Bekan may have been one of the sturdy pagans who left the Hebrides and went to Iceland, because they were disgusted at finding themselves surrounded by people who had embraced Christianity.

Still, however much Gaelic may have been influenced by Norse; it is the language of the Highlanders now, and according to the last census it is the only speech of over four thousand people in Inverness-shire.

It is an interesting fact that when a race, comparatively few in number, conquers a country and does not exterminate the people, the conquerors gradually adopt the language of the conquered people. This happened in Normandy. The Northmen conquered that province of France in 912. In a hundred and fifty years they had forgotten Norse, and were speaking French. The Normans conquered England in 1066, and in a generation or two they had forgotten French, and were speaking English. Exactly the same thing has happened in the Western Isles ; the Norse conquerors forgot Norse, and Gaelic became the language alike of conquerors and of conquered.

III. The numerous engraved stones, and articles of metal work, such as brooches and sword hilts, of undoubted Norwegian workmanship, which have been found in the Highlands and Islands, bear eloquent witness to the fact that the Norsemen were settled there in early times, and show the high level of workmanship to which their artists had attained. Doctor Henderson describes, in more or less detail, a number of these

---

* For further details on this subject I refer the reader to Dr Henderson's valuable book on " Norse Influence in Celtic Scotland."

old relics of the past, which have been found in the Hebrides, and gives illustrations of five of them. Besides these, he illustrates three Norse stone slabs found in the Isle of Man. The Norse origin of some of these is proved by the Runic inscriptions which they bear. In others it is indicated by the subjects depicted. Thor's hammer, and a pair of scales, typical of the justice of the gods, appear on some, and the Sigurd legend is represented on the Manx stones, and on one at Iona.

This old Norse story relates how Sigurd killed a huge dragon, and toasted its heart over a fire. In doing this he touched the hot dragon's heart, and, burning his finger, put it in his mouth, with the result that he immediately became possessed of " all the knowledge of the two worlds." According to another version of the same legend, it was a great serpent which he killed ; while boiling its flesh in a cauldron, the same misfortune befel him, and he adopted the same remedy, and this time he suddenly found that he understood the language of birds. On the old stones we see Sigurd engaged in combat with the dragon or the serpent, cooking the heart of the dragon, or boiling the flesh of the serpent, and putting his finger in his mouth.

In some cases the nature of the objects themselves is enough to stamp them as being of Norse origin. An image resembling old Norse idols was found near Ballachulish in 1880, and Norse swords and helmets have been found in many places. A very fine sword was found in Islay, a spearhead was found at St Kilda, a sword-hilt of extraordinary beauty on Eigg. Of this Dr Anderson says :—" I know of no finer or more elaborate piece of art workmanship, either in this country or in Norway." Many other similar finds have been made all over the Hebrides.

In Norway several grave mounds have been excavated, which contained the Viking ships in which their owners had been buried. The best preserved of these ships was found at Gokstad on the Oslo Fjord, and is now in the Museum at Oslo. As far as I know, very few of these mounds have been discovered in the Western Isles. One, however, at Killoran Bay, in Colonsay, was excavated by Mr Galloway in 1882. The

Vikings' ship had rotted away, but the nails, with which it had been constructed, were there, and the following objects were also found :—The Viking's skeleton, that of his horse, some cross-marked stones, an iron sword, and some coins, two of Eandred, 808-840, and two of Wigmund, Archbishop of York, 831-854. These last make it probable that the Viking buried here lived in the latter half of the ninth century.

Among the most interesting relics of the Norse occupation are some brooches. One was found in a Norse grave mound on Eigg ; it is a bronze brooch, silvered over. Another of quite extraordinary beauty was brought to light at West Kilbride, in Ayrshire. It is known as the Hunterston Brooch, and Professor Stephens refers to it as "Scotland's finest fibula."

Besides these things, which are certainly of Norse origin, are many others, generally believed to be Celtic work of the 16th century because they have been found in Celtic Scotland, but which may possibly be Norse work of a much earlier period. One of the most interesting of these is the old horn preserved at Dunvegan. On the silver rim of this are seven medallions. A very curious pattern appears in three. Weird animals which are often seen in undoubted Norse work, are depicted on three ; and on the seventh, where the join comes, half the pattern and a curiously-shaped animal are portrayed. Professor Brögge, head of the Museum of Antiquities at Oslo in Norway says :—"Without hesitation this is Norse work of the Island variety dating from the 10th century."

It is not very easy to describe the pattern. It appears to represent, in stone or metal, a number of long narrow strips arranged in a series of curves, and passing under or over each other where they meet. It was first met with in Russia in the fifth century, and it appeared a little later in every country in Europe. It is a marked feature in some antiquities, supposed to date from the seventh century, which were found quite lately at Abingdon, in England. It was certainly a favourite with the Norse artists who were working in the Hebrides between the tenth and the twelfth centuries, for it was used in one form or another on six out of the eight objects of which

Doctor Henderson gives illustrations, and this to some extent supports Professor Brögge's opinion that the Dunvegan horn is Norse work of the tenth century.

IV. The ownership of land. At one time Skene was regarded as the most reliable authority on this subject. I shall first deal with his theories. He maintained that among the Celts there was no individual ownership at all ; the land belonged to the tribe, and the property was divided in certain proportions amongst the male branches of the family, though the principal seat of the family, together with a certain extent of property around it, was not included in the division. The Chief besides this retained a sort of right of superiority over the whole possessions of the clan, and received a proportion of the produce of the soil as an acknowledgment of chiefship.

Even this Celtic law seems to imply that the chief possessed some more or less limited rights of ownership in the lands belonging to the tribe. But they were not personal rights ; they belonged to him as the elected chief of the community.

Under the old Norse law, called the " Asaedesret," the individual was the personal owner of the land. He " held it in absolute dominion without rendering any fealty or service to any one." This is now called the " allodial tenure." Possibly some Celtic chiefs may have retained their lands after the Norse conquest, and continued to hold them under Celtic law, but the evidence is very strong that most of the land in the Hebrides in early times was owned by Norse conquerors, who held it under Norse law, and were the personal owners of their estates.

An old charter, dated 1292, tells us that Glenelg belonged to the Norse King of Man and the Isles. We know that a Norse chief named Ljotulph was in possession of Lewis, or a portion of it, in the twelfth century, and that a little later Olaf the Black, afterwards King of Man, owned at all events part of the same island. Some light is thrown on this subject by an interesting MS. history of the MacLeods which came into my hands some time ago. It was probably written by

Dr Bannatyne MacLeod, in the early nineteenth century, but I incline to the opinion that he got his information from a sixteenth century document, which is now lost. The author of this describes the possessions of Paul Baccac, otherwise known as Phaich, undoubtedly the Paal Baalkeson of the Sagas, who was killed in 1231. These included Waternish, which had originally belonged to a branch of the Nicolsons of Lewis ; Trotternish, which had originally belonged to the Clan Vic Val or Mal, a Norwegian tribe who had settled at Duntulm ; Sleat, which had previously belonged to the Clan Vic Gurimen, a Celtic tribe ; and Snizort, part of which had been church land, while part had belonged to the Clan Vic Varten (now known as Martin). He also owned Harris, the north part of which, the Frith or Chase, had been possessed by the Clan Vic Shittich, the centre by the Clan Vic Varrachie, and the south by the MacCrimmons, who afterwards became the famous pipers of the MacLeods. " All these different tribes had been subdued by Paal's ancestors, and acknowledged his authority. Remnants of each of these are still to be met with in the country, and some of their descendants are now men of wealth and position in other parts of the world." If such large tracts of land, on the mainland, in Skye, and in the Long Island, were owned by Norsemen, probably much other land in the islands belonged to them also, and indeed the place-names point to this having been the case.

It is often maintained that the Highland chiefs wrongfully got possession of their estates when the feudal system came in, getting charters from the king to themselves of the estates which really belonged to their clans. I am, however, myself convinced that, by the beginning of the thirteenth century, the Norse laws, which governed the ownership of land, had been incorporated in the code of law under which the West Highlanders lived, and that, under this law, all the chiefs were personal owners of their estates. If this be true, the charge that they unfairly obtained possession of the property falls to the ground, for the land had been the personal property of their ancestors long before the establishment of the feudal system. This view of the status of a Highland chief in regard to his property is entirely borne out by the rules of succession which have prevailed amongst the West Highland clans from the earliest times.

V. The Norse law of succession may be briefly summed up. The eldest son always succeeded his father, and, if there was no son, a daughter was allowed to succeed. I have not been able to ascertain what rules governed the appointment of a guardian to a minor under Norse law. According to Skene, very different laws governed the succession in Celtic communities. There are four of these :

1. " There can be little doubt that among the Celts the chiefship was hereditary in the family, but elective in the individual. That is, a member of the ruling family must always be chosen, but which member of that family was to be chief was settled at a meeting of the tribe, generally held before the death of the reigning chief."

2. " In choosing a chief, under the law of tanistry, ' a brother of the ruling chief was preferred to a son, on the ground that he was one degree nearer the original founder of the family.' "

3. " If the heir who ought to succeed, and would have been elected, was under age the nearest male relation succeeded, and retained the chiefship during his life, although the proper heir had in the meantime attained his majority."

4. " Females are altogether excluded from the succession either to the chiefship or the property."

I have taken these laws which governed Celtic succession from Skene's *Highlanders of Scotland*, and have indeed quoted his own words. If the West Highland clans had been purely Celtic communities, and their lands had belonged to the tribe in accordance with Celtic custom, we should expect to find these laws of succession being observed among them. As a matter of fact we find none of them.

1. Among the West Highlanders the office of chief was certainly not elective. The eldest son, or, failing a son of the deceased chief, either a daughter or the nearest male heir

always became chief. But he did not take up the rights to
which his birth entitled him until he had been formally
accepted by the clan. In the MS., from which I have already
quoted, is an interesting account of the instalment of a chief.
It reads :—" After the funeral of the late chief all the clan
present sat down to a funeral feast. At this it was the duty
of the bards to rehearse the genealogy of the deceased, to
praise his achievements, and to lament his loss. It was then
their duty to give an exordium on the qualities of his successor,
and express the expectations of the clan as to his valour and
other virtues. This done the new chief rose in his place and
demanded his father's sword. This was always placed in his
hand by the first man in the clan, and then the new chief was
hailed by the acclamation of all present as their leader in
peace and war." It is possible that this ceremony may have
been mistaken by some writers for an election.

2. I am not aware that among West Highland clans a
brother was ever preferred to a son. A search in the pedi-
grees of West Highland families has revealed no single case of
a brother being so preferred to a son. The phrase becomes
almost monotonous : " He was succeeded by his eldest son."

3. In the MacLeod history, the family with whose records
I am better acquainted than with those of any other, there
are several instances, one as early as the fourteenth century,
of a son who was a minor succeeding, and the authority as
chief being exercised by a " tutor," generally an uncle of the
young chief, and this tutor invariably surrendered his office
when the chief attained his majority. I have no doubt that
similar instances could be adduced from the history of other
families.

4. Several instances can be given of an heiress succeeding
to an estate when she had no brother, her husband becoming
the chief. About 1340, the daughter and sole heiress of
Nicolson of Assynt married Torquil MacLeod of Lewis,
and carried the estate into the Lewis family. About 1385
Janet and Isabel, daughters and co-heiresses of John de
Ergadia, married two brothers, Sir John and Sir Robert
Stewart, and brought the Lordship of Lorn into the Stewart
family. About 1469, Isabel, daughter of Sir John Stewart,

carried the same lordship into the Argyll family, having married the Earl of Argyll. Isabel was the heiress because her brother was illegitimate, but her father at the close of his life had actually legitimised him by marrying his mother. The story of this marriage is a tragic one. As the bridal procession was entering the church, Sir John was stabbed by some one who had an interest in preventing the marriage. Though mortally wounded, Sir John was able to go through the ceremony, and his son was legitimised. But there was a slur on his birth, and that enabled Argyll to make good his claim to the Lordship of Lorn. These cases are sufficient to show that, in West Highland practice, females were not " altogether excluded from the succession."

On the other hand, when William, ninth Chief of MacLeod, died in 1553, the clan absolutely refused to acknowledge the claims of his daughter Mary, who later on married Campbell of Castle Swinny. The efforts of Argyll, her guardian, to obtain the estates for her signally failed, and she finally resigned her claim, her uncle becoming Chief, and obtaining possession of the estate. This shows that, while the succession of females was sanctioned by West Highland usage, it was not invariably allowed. I think that probably each case was decided on its merits, the personal popularity of the heiress and her husband, the character of the next male heir, and such matters as these, being important factors in the decision which was arrived at.

If Skene's theories are correct, the laws which governed the ownership of land and the succession to dignities amongst the West Highlanders were very important results of the Norse occupation.

But Skene is no longer accepted by learned men as an infallible authority on these subjects. In 1921, Professor John MacNeill, a very distinguished historian, published a book, entitled " Celtic Ireland." Unfortunately, I do not possess a copy of this work, and it is not among the books in the only public library to which I have access. Therefore, I have not been able to make myself acquainted with the conclusions at which Professor MacNeill has arrived. But

a learned friend writes concerning this book as follows :—
" The author has a chapter on the ownership of land, in which
he deals with the tribal and communal ideas, and explodes
them.   He has another chapter on the Irish law of succession.
His work quite supersedes previous treatment.   It is work
which could be done only by an Irishman who really knows
the country and its early literature."

Now that Skene's theories have been discredited, it is
possible that the Norse influence in forming the land laws
and rules of succession which prevailed in the West Highlands
may have been less strong than I previously supposed.   But
considering how closely the Norse and West Highland codes
of law resembled each other, I think that probably the latter
was to a great extent derived from the former, and that in
this, as in other matters, the Norse influence was very strong.

But if the Norsemen profoundly influenced the Celts in
many directions, the Celts also exercised a great influence
over the Norsemen.   As has been already pointed out, the
language of the Celts, as somewhat modified by Norse influence, became the speech of the West Highlanders.   I
incline to the opinion that the belief in fairies and water-
kelpies, in magic and witchcraft, which was so firmly held
amongst our ancestors, is mainly due to the Celts, for it
is clear that they were a much more imaginative people
than the Norsemen.   The "frith," which was a kind of
divination used in the Highlands to discover the where-
abouts of an absent person, and which was also an incanta-
tion by which a person could be made invisible, may have
been learnt from the Norsemen.   The Sutherland traditions
which describe the way in which " Fearchar Leiche," the
Gaelic name of the famous physician Beaton, obtained his
marvellous powers of diagnosing and healing disease, is
clearly derived from the Norse story of Sigurd, which I have
already related.   Probably some other Highland superstitions may be traced to a Norse origin, but on the whole I
think that the imaginative side of the West Highlander's
character is mainly derived from his Celtic ancestors.

Undoubtedly the most important gift which the Celts
bequeathed to their descendants was their religion.   They

had been Christians for something like 300 years, when the Norse settled amongst them, having learnt the truths of Christianity from St Columba and his disciples. On the other hand, the Norse invaders were worshippers of Odin, Freya, and of all the gods of Valhalla. They were inspired by an intense hatred of the White Christ, and how, or when, these enemies of Christ became His servants, we cannot tell with any certainty. The influence of the Christians amongst whom they lived no doubt had a great effect, and in course of time the Norsemen in the Hebrides forsook the service of their old gods, and accepted Christianity.

Thus, slowly and by degrees, during the tenth, eleventh, and twelfth centuries, the Celts and the Norsemen, living together, marrying with each other, influencing each other in many ways, were drawing closer and closer together, and by the beginning of the thirteenth century the two races had been welded into one, and, to some extent, the Norse element had been absorbed in the Celtic. But it must not be forgotten that the West Highlanders of to-day are a hybrid race, and that, while they owe much to their Celtic forebears, they also owe much to the hardy Norsemen who ruled over the Isles for 400 years.

CHAPTER II.

THE CLAN SYSTEM.

COMPARISON WITH THE PATRIARCHAL AND FEUDAL
SYSTEMS—THE CHIEFS, THE CHIEFTAINS, THE RANK
AND FILE—THE GOVERNMENT OF A CLAN—ITS MILI-
TARY ORGANISATION—THE MUTUAL LOVE OF CLANS-
MEN FOR EACH OTHER.

A West Highland clan was not governed by the laws of
the realm, but by the Chief, and by the Chieftains who acted
under his authority. At first, no doubt, he assumed that the
administration of justice was part of his duty as Chief. Later,
when he got charters from the Crown, very extensive powers
were expressly granted to him. I quote the words of one
charter : " Cum furca " (gallows), " fossa " (the pit in which
a female felon was drowned), " Sac et Soc " (rights of jurisdiction), " infang thef " (jurisdiction over a thief taken in his
own bounds), " outfang thef " (jurisdiction over a thief taken
outside his bounds). These were the heritable jurisdictions which the Chiefs possessed and exercised till they
were taken away by the Act of 1747. They conferred on him
absolute authority over all his clansmen, including the power
of life and death.

In war, as in peace, the Chief was supreme. He super-
intended the training of his men in the art of war ; he commanded them in every campaign ; he led them personally
into the thick of the battle, and shared all the perils of warfare with the humblest of his followers.

No class of men have ever had more varied duties to perform
or carried on their shoulders a heavier load of responsibility
than the mediaeval Chiefs. On their capacity as statesmen,
diplomatists, and soldiers, the very existence of their clans
often depended, and their kindness of heart, good sense, and
sound judgment could alone secure the happiness and well-
being of their people.

No doubt there were some bad Chiefs who grossly mis-used their power, and treated their clansmen with great harshness and cruelty, but the evidence is very strong that most of them were the kind and beneficent friends of their people.

One very remarkable instance of their solicitude for the welfare of their clansmen has come down to us. The Chiefs took steps to secure for their people when wounded or in bad health the benefit of medical attendance. It is recorded that a great many of them gave a farm rent free to a medical man on condition that he attended to their clansmen.

Most of the doctors who were thus employed belonged to the distinguished family of the Beatons, lairds of Balfour. The members of this family possessed the gift of healing in a very remarkable degree, and numbers of them were settled in the Highlands from remote times. Several medical works in Gaelic by some of this family are in the National Library of Scotland.

As early as 1379, Farquhar Beaton received the lands of Melness and Hope in Sutherland from Prince Alexander Stewart. Another Beaton settled on the Argyll estate in the fifteenth century. One Fergus Beaton was physician to the Lord of the Isles in 1448, and also became Chancellor of the Isles. In the same century a member of this family settled on the MacLeod estate in Skye, and was given the farm of Summerdale, in Bracadale. Another Beaton, in the following century, was given the lands of Pennycross, in Mull, by Mac-Lean of Duart.

This custom endured as long as the clan system lasted. In the Dunvegan Estate accounts of the 18th century are many entries of payments being made to doctors and nurses, and several letters show that at the same time the Chief was caring for the welfare of his people in another direction. Whenever the crops failed at home he used to charter vessels to bring food into the country, spending large sums of money, and often finding the greatest difficulty in carrying out his beneficent intentions.

It is quite certain that, though the Chiefs exercised absolute power over their people, they were generally kind and benevolent despots.

The consequence of this, and the best proof that it is true, is that they were loved. There can be no doubt about this. Skene quotes from a letter, written by an officer of engineers in 1750, some very remarkable words :—" The ordinary Highlanders esteem it the most supreme degree of virtue to love their Chief, and pay him blind obedience."

Martin Martin says that the people said grace before and after meals, and that they always added a petition to God for their Chief's welfare. Even as late as 1777, the tenants on the MacLeod estate, " out of their personal affection for the Chief," at a time when he was in serious financial difficulties, came forward and offered to pay an increased rent for their farms. Fear may be given to a cruel despot, but Love is not given where it is not deserved, and the mere fact that the Chiefs were loved, shows that they were not unworthy of their people's affection.

The Chiefs, living in their castles, maintained an almost Royal establishment. Each of them always had in attendance a number of the gentlemen of his clan—in old days probably a great many, but an order of Council, made in 1616, fixes the number which the different Chiefs might keep in their household. MacLean of Duart, who seems to have been considered the most important of the Island Chiefs, was allowed eight ; MacLeod and Clan Ranald six each, the MacLeans of Coll and Lochbuy, and MacKinnon, three each.

An entry in some seventeenth century accounts at Dunvegan shows that the wives of the Chiefs had ladies-in-waiting in attendance. This entry records the fact that £4 0s 0d a year was paid to " My lady's gentlewoman." In the Inverness-shire Valuation Roll, dated 1644, a note is given as to the titles borne by ladies of different degrees of rank. " The wife of the owner of a barony is called ' Lady,' such as Lady Glenmorrison ; the wife of a landowner of respectable standing was called ' good wife,' such as good wife of Suddie ; the wife of the humble order of landowner was called ' Mistress,' such as ' the mistress of Kinchyle.' "

Besides these gentlemen, the Chief always had in his household a numerous band of retainers, and, when he went out, was attended by a body-guard composed of the bravest men in his clan.

They continued to maintain this semi-Royal state as long as the clan system lasted. Writing of them at the end of the seventeenth century, Macaulay describes them as follows :— " Within the four seas and less than six hundred miles from London, were many miniature courts, in each of which a petty prince, attended by guards, by armour-bearers, by musicians, by an hereditary orator, by an hereditary poet laureate, kept a rude state, dispensed a rude justice, waged wars, and concluded treaties."

One curious custom which was in vogue amongst the Chiefs during several centuries may be noticed here. They used frequently, if not habitually, to entrust the care of a son to foster parents, to be " Fosterit, interteinit, maintenet and upbroucht ay and quhil. he be apt for schoolis. God always spaireing him dayis and lyfe." The words quoted appear in a contract of fosterage dated 1637, which is preserved at Dunvegan.

Two possible reasons occur to me for this custom. The Chief may have feared that his castle might be captured by an enemy, and all its inhabitants put to the sword. If this should happen, his son, living with foster parents at a distance from his home, would be safe. Or he may have realised that in his own home could not be found a suitable atmosphere in which to bring up a boy. His son would certainly receive from the clansmen, who crowded his castle, an amount of adulation and flattery which would not be good for him ; while the hard-drinking guests, who so frequently sat at his table, would set the boy a bad example, and very possibly lead him into habits which might be fatal to him.

Next in importance to the Chief in every clan were the men whom Skene calls " The heads of houses," and who at a later period were known as " tacksmen." When writing of them in early days it will be more accurate to give them the title which they formerly bore, and call them " Chieftains."

These men combined in their own persons a great variety of offices. They were tenant farmers, magistrates, officers in the army, and privy councillors.

Each one of them in his own domain was a petty king. His dependants varied in rank from his own kinsmen, the " duine uaisle," down to the bondmen, who had been called in very early times the " nativi," but all owed him absolute obedience. When the clan was at peace he was responsible for the government of his people, and for the military training of his men ; when it was at war, he commanded his unit on the field of battle.

The amount of land held by the Chieftains varied in extent. Some might occupy a farm which would in modern days be rented at £300 a year, on which 30 or 40 families lived ; the holdings of others might not be more than half this in extent, value, or population. For their farms they paid rent to the Chiefs.

The Chieftains also had to render certain services. Their first and most important duty was to come themselves, and bring all their men, to join the martial array of the clan whenever the Chief called them out to battle. When one of them died, a fine was payable to his superior, and a " herezeld," the best animals on the farm, was exacted. When a Chief's daughter married, and possibly on some other occasions, extra payments were claimed. They were bound to receive the Chief and his household as guests whenever he chose to pay them a visit, and to give anyone he liked to quarter on them free board and lodging for unlimited periods of time. These guests were called " Sorners." This word is supposed to be a corruption of sojourners.

The more important Chieftains were members of the Chief's Privy Council, and settled with him such questions as peace or war, and the attitude which he should take up towards other clans, or toward the government in Edinburgh. Some of them were always in attendance on the Chief, not only that their presence might help to maintain his dignity, but also that some members of the Council might be always on the spot to advise him in any unforeseen emergency which might arise. Macaulay, while admitting the ignorance, as far as book-learning goes, which prevailed among these men, pays a high tribute to their ability and capacity as statesmen in the following words :—" It is probable that in the High-land Councils, men, who would not have been qualified for the duty of parish clerks, sometimes argued questions of peace and war, of tribute and homage, with an ability worthy of Halifax or Carmarthen."

The rank and file of a clan, the immediate dependents of a chief, and those of each chieftain, lived under conditions which closely resembled those that prevailed under the Patri-archal system. A superior looked on his dependents as mem-bers of his family rather than as his servants, he accepted full responsibility for their welfare, and he recognised that it was, as much his duty to maintain them, as it was to support his own children.

They rendered to him all manner of services ; they fol-lowed him to the field of battle, they cultivated his fields, they tended his cattle, they looked after his horses, they clipped his sheep, they spun his wool, they wove his cloth, they made his butter and cheese, they cut his peats, they went out to catch fish for him, they did every odd job he required. In return for all the services which they rendered they were paid no wages, but they received maintenance for themselves and their families.

Their master gave them the corn, the wool, the milk, all that I may call the raw material from which their needs could be supplied, and, in their own time, they worked up the raw material into the finished products ; the meal, the clothes, the butter and the cheese. And all this work each family did for itself. As they were not their superior's whole-time em-ployees, when he did not require their services, they could do work for themselves, and, since each of those whom they served had a large number of men on his farm, probably they had a great deal of time at their own disposal.

I have not been able to ascertain whether there was any system of small holdings in existence in early days or not. It is possible that each man held a plot of ground which he could call his own, and which he cultivated for the maintenance of himself and his family, but I incline to the contrary opinion, and I think that on each farm the family life was being lived on a larger scale.

Just as the sons and daughters of a modern farmer give their services to work their father's farm and receive no wages for doing so, but are boarded, lodged and clothed free of cost, so the dependants of a Chief or Chieftain received no wages, but were maintained by their master. I believe that, on the whole, this system worked well and that, in the six centuries during which it endured, the people were happy and contented with their lot.

One result necessarily followed under this system. Receiving no wages, they had no means of paying others to do anything for them. In early days there was no sub-division of labour. There were no tailors, no shoemakers, no tanners, no weavers, no mills in which corn could be ground, no shops in which necessaries could be bought. Each family supplied its own needs by its own labour, in other words, each was a self-sufficing unit in the clan.

These were the outstanding features of the patriarchal system. Living ourselves under such different conditions it is difficult for us to realise what such a mode of life meant. Each one of us renders some service to others, and is paid for doing so ; with the money we earn we buy the food, the clothing, the fuel, the light, and all the other things we require. We make none of them. Our forbears had to make all of them, or go without.

One most remarkable feature of the Clan system remains to be noted. I have already dwelt on the love which the people gave to their Chief. The Officer of Engineers, whom Skene quotes, says that all the members of a clan had a deep affection for each other. I give his words—" Next to this love of their Chief is that of their own particular branch "—that is, I suppose, of their own Chieftain—" and, in a third degree, to those of the whole clan, whom they will assist, right or wrong, against those of any other tribes with whom they are at variance."

In these words he shows an extraordinarily attractive picture of what clan life and clan feeling were in the old days.

It is a remarkable fact that this clan feeling and this devotion to the Chief still survive. Whether they live in Scotland, or Canada, or Australia, or New Zealand, fellow-clansmen feel that they are all members of a great brotherhood ; they take a keen interest in the records of the past, which tell of the heroic deeds which their forbears did ; they make pilgrimages to the old country, that they may see the places where their forefathers lived, and search in the old kirk-yards for the moss-covered stones which tell where they lie ; and, when they meet a fellow-clansman, they receive him with open arms, and treat him as a brother. We might have expected that, in these practical utilitarian days, such sentiments would be forgotten and die out. As a matter of fact, the letters which I am constantly receiving from fellow-clansmen all over the world, convince me that they are growing stronger every day. Curiously enough, as I wrote the last sentence, the evening post came in, and, among my letters, was one from a brother clansman in America.

Having briefly sketched the main features of the clan system, I now proceed to consider its origin.

As has been already explained, during the four centuries which followed the coming of the Norsemen to the Syderies, the two races, the Celts and the Scandinavians, were slowly amalgamating. Towards the end of the twelfth century, or early in the thirteenth, the fusion was complete. Then, and not till then, the History of the West Highland Clans may be said to begin. It is true that the Chiefs could trace their descent from Celtic or Norse Kings and potentates who lived at a much earlier period ; it is also true that their clansmen were descended from men of both races who had been living in the country for centuries ; but it was at the period I have named that the clan system was finally evolved out of the conditions which preceded its formation.

Many theories have been propounded as to the nature and origin of the Clan system. Two of these require careful consideration. The first is the theory set forth by Skene in his " Highlanders of Scotland." He thought that the extraordinary love and devotion, which the clansmen gave to their chiefs, could only be accounted for by the assumption that there was blood relationship between them. He therefore held that the clan system was identical with the patriarchal, and that a Chief and his people were all descended from a common ancestor.

I think that Skene was mistaken, both in his premise and his conclusion. In the first place, blood relationship has certainly not been always the close bond of union which he imagines it to have been, and it is certain that other ties, such as the loyalty of a people to their Sovereign, or the devotion of servants to their masters, have often sufficed to bind together people, who were in no way connected with each other by blood, in a bond of union as close as that which united a Chief and his people.

In the second place, all the evidence we possess tends to show that Skene's theory is not tenable, at all events in the Western Isles. It is true that the men in authority were generally the Chief's kinsmen, having been placed in the positions they occupied by him, but the following considerations indicate that there was no blood relationship between the Chief and the masses of his clansmen.

(a) The details given in the first chapter as to the original possessors of the lands which afterwards were comprised in the MacLeod country, show that these lands had been held by eleven distinct tribes, that they had later been conquered by three Norse Chiefs, and finally had all of them passed into the possession of Leod, the first Chief of the MacLeods. It is quite inconceivable that the people on these eleven portions of Leod's estate can all of them have been descended from a common ancestor with him ; as a matter of fact, it is probable that none of them were, and yet they gave the most unbounded devotion to him and to his successors.

(b) A great deal of land in the West Highlands was being transferred from one family to another during the fourteenth and fifteenth centuries. I mentioned several cases in the first chapter, and many others could be adduced. The new Chief may have put his own relations and friends in positions of authority on his recently-acquired territory, but the mass of the old inhabitants remained. In only one instance, when the Campbells acquired the Lordship of Lorn, was there " a great flitting " (we are not told where the people went to). In all the other cases, not only did the people remain, but, at all events after a short time, they gave the same devotion to their new Lords which they had given to their old ones, and, in a generation or two, forgot that there had ever been any change at all. It is impossible to suppose that these people and their new Chief can have been descended from a common ancestor.

(c) Belonging to each great Clan were a number of small tribes, called " minor septs." These, probably to obtain the protection which a powerful Chief could give, had attached themselves to the Clan, and acknowledged the authority of its head. There could be no possibility of blood relationship between him and these distinct tribes, and yet history tells us that these minor septs were as devoted to their Chief as any of those who bore his name, and really were his kin.

What, then, was the true origin of the Clan system ? I am convinced that the foundation on which the Clan system rested was not the descent of the Chief and his people from a common ancestor, but the fact that he owned the land on which they lived. A 13th century Chief, holding his estate under the Norse land laws, was the personal owner of his land, and all the people who lived on that land were his dependants. If any change in ownership took place, the people passed under the authority of a new Lord. This appears to me to be the only possible deduction from the facts I have given above. But though the two systems, the Clan and the Patriarchal, differed from each other in their origin, they were precisely similar in their effects, and it may be said with truth that, during six centuries, the West High-landers lived under conditions which in their nature were purely Patriarchal, and which may correctly be described as such.

According to a second theory, which has been strongly maintained by some writers, the Clan system is for all practical purposes identical with the feudal system. This, I believe, became true towards the end of the 13th century, but it must not be forgotten that the origin of the two systems was entirely different. Under the feudal system, theoretically all the land in a country belongs to the King, and the estate which a feudal Baron held had been granted to him by the Crown, certain specified services being reserved in the charter.

A West Highland estate came into existence in a very different way. Originally it had been occupied by some one at a very remote time, then it had been conquered, perhaps it had been conquered several times, and the owner in the thirteenth century may have derived it by descent from the original occupier, or from one of the conquerors ; or he may have married an heiress ; but it is certain that he had never received any grant of it from a King, and that, as he held it under the Norse land laws, as a land owner he was subject to no superior, and was not called upon to render any service for his land to any one.

But in 1266, Magnus, King of Norway, ceded the Western Isles to Scotland, and the most important result which followed on this event was the change in the laws under which land was held in the Islands.

Alexander III., after he had added the Islands to his dominion, introduced the feudal system. He created four great Baronies, and all the land in the Islands was included in one or other of these. The four Barons were the Earl of Ross, Angus Macdonald of Islay, Allan MacRuari of Garmovan and the North Isles, and John de Ergadia, the Lord of Lorne.

This did not mean that the Chiefs, who had owned land in the Western Isles before they were ceded to Scotland, were ejected from their estates. Their rights had been protected in the treaty under which the cession was made ; and, indeed, as it is important to remember, the grant of a barony never confiscated the lands of those who were in the possession of estates within its boundaries. It merely put them under the authority of a new Lord. Neither did it mean that the independence of a Chief within his own bounds was curtailed. He continued to manage his estate, and to govern his clansmen, just as he had done before.

But it did mean that henceforth these Chiefs held their lands under a superior Lord, and from that time onward the clan system was really identical with the feudal system.

Another question remains to be considered. What was the position occupied by the Chiefs outside their own countries at various periods ? Before the cession of the Isles to Scotland they were subject to the King of Man and the Isles. After the cession they became subject to four superior Lords and later, when the four baronies were merged in one, to the Lord of the Isles. These superiors were resident in the country, and had ample power to enforce their rights. Therefore, we may safely assume that, unlike the King in later times, they exercised a real authority over their vassals, and that the latter were in no sense of the word independent. But they certainly occupied a great position in the world. Being in the 14th century loyal subjects of the Scottish Kings, as Fordun tells us they were, they often went south. They received there the treatment due to great and powerful nobles ; and they were welcome guests in the palace of the King. It is a remarkable fact that, in one at least of the ancient armorials, above their arms appears, not the helmet of an esquire, but one of the peculiar form allotted by the law of heraldry to princes and nobles.

At that time they often married the daughters of great Southern Lords, such as the Earls of Douglas and Mar. At a later period, when the constant rebellions of the Island Lords had severed the connections between the Lowlands and the West Highlands, we find that they married very closely among themselves. A Chief's wife was almost always the daughter of a brother Chief.

The forfeiture of the Island Lordship in 1493 brought about a great change. The Chiefs were now under the direct rule of the King, but he lived far from his island dominions, and he had all the other affairs of his realm to attend to. Consequently he was able to exert very little real authority over his vassals in the Western Isles.

During the next 120 years the Chiefs, though they owed a nominal obedience to the King, were practically independent potentates. They made war on each other without let or hindrance. They exercised all the rights of sovereign princes. They habitually and successfully defied the Royal authority. They continued to hold their estates after they had been forfeited by the King and granted to other people. They failed to appear before him to answer for their misdoings, and they refused to allow the emissaries of the law to enter their territories. The weakness of the law is illustrated by some words in a legal document at Dunvegan, dated in 1527 :— " Alexander MacLeod dwelleth in ye isles where ye Officers of ye law dare not pass for hazard of their lives." This state of affairs continued for a great many years, and during this period it is no exaggeration to say that each of the Island Chiefs was really an independent potentate.

But in 1609 the statutes of Iona were agreed to, which event will be more fully related in a later chapter. The Chiefs then submitted to the Royal authority, and the reign of law may be said to have begun in the Western Isles.

They were not all of them, however, law-abiding subjects of the King. Even as late as 1680, the law was set at nought in the Islands. In the report of a trial at Edinburgh in that year, the following story is told :—An unfortunate notary had been sent to serve a writ on MacNeill of Barra. " He proceeded, as custom is, to lay the writ at the door of the house, but the said Rory MacNeill, in high and proud contempt of His Majesty's authority, threw large stones from the roof of his house, by which the said notar was in hazard of being brained, and discharged four score shots from guns, hagbutts, pistols, muskets, and other invasive and forbidden weapons, whereby he was put in hazard of his life, and took all the papers he had in his company, and did rend and ryve the same." It is clear, however, that by this time the law was not quite powerless, for MacNeill was brought to Edinburgh and tried for this offence.

It appears that MacNeill habitually treated unwelcome guests in the manner described in this report. On a tower above the entrance to his stronghold (in Castle Bay, Barra), a windlass may still be seen. Ropes attached to this windlass were tied round the stones, which were flung on the heads of visitors, and, in this way, the stones could be hauled up, and the same missiles could be used again and again.

It must be clearly understood that when the statutes of Iona were passed, the Clan system did not come to an end.

Within their own bounds during the next 128 years the Chiefs were as powerful as they had ever been, and continued to govern their clansmen in just the same way as they had always done. The Clan system remained in full force till it was destroyed by the Heritable Jurisdictions Act of 1747.

CHAPTER III.

THE CLANSMEN.

THEIR NUMBERS—CLASSES IN A CLAN—GENTLEMEN,
SENNACHIES, LABOURERS—CHARACTER OF THE
PEOPLE, THEIR FAULTS, THEIR MUSICAL AND POETIC
GIFTS—SPORTS, HUNTING, WAR—THEIR FOOD AND
DRINK, THEIR DRESS, THEIR RELIGION—FOSTERAGE.

" One of the first objects of an enquirer, who wishes to
form a correct idea of the state of a community at a given
time, must be to ascertain of how many persons that community then consisted " (Macaulay : History, Chapter III.)

In the Highlands this is not easy, for no census was there
taken till 1851. In the following estimate I have confined my
attention to Skye, Harris and Glenelg, where I have some data
to go on, but, probably, the same causes which increased or
decreased population were equally at work all over the Highlands.

In early times there is no evidence of what the population
was. The force which a clan could put into the field at any
given time affords no clue to the population living on the Chief's
estate, for that was more a question of arms than of men. It
is not till 1772 that we find any definite statements. There is
a report of that date on Harris, preserved at Dunvegan, which
gives the population of that island at 1993, and in the same
year Pennant fixes the population of Glenelg at 700, and that
of Skye at from 12,000 to 13,000, but he says that about 1750
it may have been 15,000. This drop is probably accounted
for by some emigration which took place about 1769, the first
reference I find to emigration in any of the papers at Dunvegan.

There is no reason to suppose that in earlier days the
population was greater than it was about 1770. It was probably smaller. For centuries the clans were engaged in warfare, external or internal. These wars were carried on with
ruthless ferocity, and the loss of life which they involved
would alone suffice to keep down the numbers of the people.

Other causes were also at work. I have not been able to ascertain when small-pox first visited the Highlands, but it is certain that the disease made fearful ravages in the 17th and 18th centuries. There are many references to small-pox in letters preserved at Dunvegan, and the word Breac (spotted), which is added to the names of quite a number of people living in old days, implies that they were pitted with small-pox.

The disease in one outbreak carried off the whole population of St Kilda, except three men. One autumn these men were taken over to Boreray, one of the St Kilda group of islands, and left there to catch birds, it being arranged that a boat should return to fetch them in a week's time. The week passed, a month passed, the whole winter passed, and no boat came. They must have suffered great privations, but somehow they managed to exist during these weary months. At last they saw the factor's vessel arrive on its annual visit to St Kilda. They lit a fire, the smoke was seen, and a boat was sent for them. Then they learned what had happened. A few days after they had left the main island a ship had been wrecked, on which was a man suffering from small-pox. One by one, all the inhabitants of the island contracted the disease and died. That was the reason the three men had not been fetched, and death from small-pox was, in all human probability, the fate they had escaped. For these reasons I am convinced that the estimates which have been formed of a teeming population which inhabited our glens in ancient days are much exaggerated.

It was not until a much later period that the numbers of people living in the country became much greater. In the first half of the nineteenth century the population increased by leaps and bounds. The Duke of Argyle says, in his book, " Scotland As It Was And Is," that people whose food consists mainly of potatoes are usually very prolific, and, if this is the case, it may account for the great increase in population, both in Ireland and in the Highlands.

From some figures in a Gazeteer of Scotland, published in 1845, from a memorandum by the late MacLeod, about 1846, which gives approximately the population on different estates in the Highlands, and from the numbers Pennant gives, I have constructed the following table, which gives the population at different periods :—

	1772.	1801.	1831.	1845.	1911.
Skye	13,000	13,728	22,796	29,500	13,319
Harris	1,993	2,996	3,900	8,500	4,974
Glenelg	700	2,834	2,874	1,800	481

I cannot account for the figures in Glenelg, but I imagine that Pennant put the numbers too low in 1772, and that there was emigration between 1831 and 1845. The kelp industry probably caused the increase in Harris, but I have reason to believe that the number given in 1846 was too high. The rise between 1801 and 1831 took place in spite of the fact that in 1811 a great many tacksmen emigrated, taking some of their farm labourers with them. But there was no wholesale emigration till after the potato famine, when it became necessary that more than half the people should seek a livelihood in other lands. This emigration accounts for the great drop between 1845 and 1911. The subject of emigration will be further dealt with in Chapter VIII.

In the following pages I shall very frequently refer to Martin Martin. In 1707 he published an " Account of the Western Isles," which is a mine of information on the manners and customs of the Islanders, their methods of government, the dress they wore, and their personal characters. He was himself a Highlander ; he was governor to the Laird of MacLeod's children, and lived for many years at Dunvegan. He was a keen observer, and deeply interested in his subject. He is the earliest, and in many ways the most instructive, of all those who have written on the Western clans, and the reader will find that I have made many quotations from his book.

There were no doubt many gradations of rank in a Highland clan, as in other communities, but, broadly speaking, we may divide the clansmen into two classes, the gentlemen " quhilkis labouris not the ground," as the report of 1590 calls them, and the humbler classes, who did labour the ground. The first class included the Chiefs, the Chieftains, the members of their families, and the more important office-bearers in the

Chief's household, the harpers, pipers, bards, seannachies and standard bearers.

They were the aristocracy of the Islands. Though they did no manual work, they certainly did not lead inactive lives. Some of them were educated for the priesthood. The Mac-Kinnons, who appear to have been the most ecclesiastically-minded family in the Isles, produced more than one Bishop, and one or two Abbots of Iona. One of the MacLeod Chiefs, having intended to take Holy Orders, is always spoken of as " an cleireach," the clerk, and the names of many dignitaries of the Church, who belonged to one or other of the leading families in the Highlands, are mentioned in history.

Even in those early days the management of a farm required some knowledge of how the land should be tilled, and of how live stock should be treated. Moreover. the operations of those who actually " laboured the ground " had to be directed, and the sons of a Chieftain must have received some instruction on such matters during their youth, and devoted some time to such avocations as they grew older.

But undoubtedly war was the main occupation pursued by members of this class. From their earliest childhood they were trained in the use of arms ; as they grew up they became the officers who instructed the youth of the clan in the art of war, and led them out to the field of battle. On their valour and efficiency the safety of a clan often depended ; and, though they did not labour the ground, it cannot be denied that they played a very important part in securing the welfare of the clan to which they belonged.

But the existence of a purely military class in any community is always a danger, and it is likely that the influence of these men brought about many of the disastrous feuds in which the clans were plunged at one time in their history.

It is not easy to ascertain what percentage of the population belonged to this class. If all the descendants of early gentle-folk claimed the privilege through the centuries, their numbers must have been very large ; but I imagine that they did not generally do so. The Banatyne MS. mentions several families which " had been once powerful, but the members of which, while they retained their pride of birth, had become no more

3

than peasants." Moreover, the gentlemen of a clan took part
in every war, and as the officers of an army always lose more
heavily in a campaign than the rank and file, losses on the
field of battle must have kept down their numbers. It is also
certain that some of the gentlemen of the Isles sought an
outlet for their energies in foreign lands. About 1390 a
younger son of the Dunvegan Chief migrated to Lorraine,
where he founded a family of some distinction, representatives
of which are still living in Canada. A little later some West
Highlanders were to be found in the Scottish Guards of the
French King. Later still, when employment in warlike enterprises was no longer to be found at home, large numbers of
them took service in Holland, Sweden, Germany, and wherever
mercenary troops were employed in the wars of the time.   I
incline to the opinion that between eight and ten per cent.
of the population were of gentle birth.

A very important class in every clan was that to which
the seannachies and bards belonged.   These men were
historians and genealogists. There were hereditary seannachies
in the household of every Chief, and it was their business
to learn from their fathers all the records of the past, to
recite them at the banquets in their Lord's hall, and to
hand them down to their descendants.   Their knowledge
was very rarely committed to paper until comparatively
recent times, and some writers hold that the traditions,
which have come down to us, are without any value for
historical purposes.

But three circumstances are worthy of consideration.   In
the first place, the seannachies were trained men.   It appears
that there were colleges in Ireland, where history and genealogy were taught, and that many of our Highland bards and
seannachies had been educated at these seats of learning.
Secondly, just as John Barbour put his history of " the Brus "
into metrical form, so the old Highland traditions were put
into the form of poems. This made it easier to remember
them, and though it did not prevent a fraudulent bard
from interpolating spurious matter of his own, it made it less
likely that he should do so accidentally.   In the third place,
the bards and seannachies not only had to recite their effusions

before chiefs and clansmen, who would be unlikely to detect any errors they might make, but also in the presence of other bards and seannachies, who would be perfectly capable of doing so, and who, as there was a great deal of jealousy amongst these men, would certainly not allow them to pass unchallenged.

These considerations induce me to believe that, in the old traditions which have come down to us, we have more or less trustworthy records of events which really did take place in the past.

The upper classes in the West Highlands possessed many great and remarkable virtues, but they suffered from one very serious failing. They were much addicted to strong drink. Their Norse ancestors had certainly not been averse to deep potations, and they probably inherited from them the taste for strong drink. We know that in the seventeenth century great quantities of wine and brandy were being brought into the country, and that the drinking was very heavy. So serious was the evil that the Secret Council had to interfere, and limit the amount of wine which each Chief might import. It is quite likely that, in earlier centuries, the same custom prevailed, and that wine and brandy were imported from France. Possibly then also there may have been the same excessive drinking among the Chiefs and Chieftains, who could afford to buy these expensive refreshments.

But there is no evidence that there was any drunkenness among the poorer classes. They certainly could not afford to drink imported wine or brandy. They brewed some ale or mead from barley for their own use, but, my informant tells me, it was non-intoxicating. Spirits were not distilled in the country till some time in the seventeenth century. Martin Martin says that in his time " their drink was water," and I think it more than likely that they had been equally abstemious in earlier days.

I imagine that the upper classes were well and plentifully fed. Each autumn, " marts," as the beasts used for this purpose were called, were killed and salted down for use in the winter, so they had plenty of beef. But Martin Martin tells us that the humbler classes " ate very little meat. Their food was butter, milk, cheese, brochan (porridge), colworts, and bread." Colworts are a kind of cabbage, and this implies that they grew these vegetables. The bread was probably either oatcake or barley cakes, perhaps both. This can scarcely be called luxurious fare, but they seem to have thriven on it very well. Martin goes on to say that they were " healthy and vigorous, and capable of strenuous and pro-longed exertion by land and sea," and in a report concerning the men whom the Lord of the Isles took to Ireland in 1545 to co-operate with the troops of Henry VIII. in a campaign in that country, they are described as " very tall men."

It is somewhat curious that fish is not included among the articles of food which, according to Martin, the Islesmen ate. They were certainly not ardent fishermen, but I imagine that they did catch and consume fish in the old days.

They were clad in the same dress as the one their ancestors had worn from time immemorial. The extreme antiquity of the costume is absolutely proved by the fact that Highlanders are to be seen wearing such a dress on many old crosses and tomb-stones in different parts of the country. Among these are the crossses at Dupplin and Nigg, both of which probably date from the ninth century, MacMillan's cross at Kilmory in Knapdale dating from the fourteenth century, and a Mac-Leod tomb-stone at Iona, probably of the same date. It may be noted also that Magnus, King of Norway, got the surname of " Barefoot," because, after he returned from his expedition to the Isles in 1093, he adopted the dress which was then being worn by his Hebridean subjects.

Three early writers describe the dress as it was worn in their own times—John Major (1512), Bishop Leslie (1578), and Martin Martin (1707). From their accounts of it I shall try to obtain a clear idea concerning the evolution of the kilt as we know it.

Its earliest form was the " lenicroich." In this, kilt, waistcoat and coat were combined in one. It was a strip of linen 18 yards long ; the breadth is not mentioned ; the por-tion which went round the waist was " stitched in many folds," and secured in its place by a belt. Like our kilt, it fell as far as the knees. The rest of the garment was draped round the body, and fastened on the breast with a " bodkin of bone or wood." The lenicroichs worn by the gentlemen were yellow in colour, being dyed with saffron ; those worn by the humbler classes were " painted or daubed with pitch." This was probably the only garment worn by all classes in summer.

The lenicroich, being made of linen, was not very warm, so in cold weather the common people covered it with deerskin, while the gentlemen wore " a mantle " over it. This was undoubtedly the garment which we call a plaid. It is described by Bishop Leslie in 1578 as " long and flowing, but capable of being neatly gathered up at pleasure into folds." Bishop Leslie also says that in his time " both nobles and common people wore mantles of one sort, except that the nobles preferred those of different colours," probably tartans. I gather from this that by his time the common people had given up covering their linen garment with deerskin, and had taken to wearing plaids, but theirs, it is clear, were not tartan plaids. Such was the Highland dress down to the end of the 16th century.

Martin tells us that about the year 1607 a new form of the costume was evolved. Wool was the material used instead of linen. This being much warmer, it was unnecessary to wear anything over it, even in winter, and the mantle or plaid became the upper part of the one garment which was now worn. This was called the "breakan or plaid." The plaid does not mean here the robe we call by that name, but the single garment, which included kilt, coat, waistcoat, and plaid in one. Martin thus describes it : " It was made of fine wool of divers colours, its length is commonly seven double ells. It is tied on the breast with a bodkin of bone or wood ; it is pleated from the belt to the knee very nicely." I gather from this that it was a reproduction of the lenicroich in cloth, a good deal heavier, because the material was thicker, and including four parts of the modern dress instead of three. The division of the one garment into four probably took place in the 18th century.

The descriptions given by different authorities as to what our forefathers wore on their heads, legs and feet,

differ a good deal.   " D'Arteille, the French Ambassador,
who accompanied James V. on his Hebridean voyage in 1540,
says " they go with their heads bare, and allow their hair to
grow very long, and they wear neither stockings nor shoes,
except some who wear buskins, made in a very old fashion,
which come as high as their knees."   But Martin says, " the
shoes anciently worn were pieces of the hide of a cow, horse
or deer, with the hair on, being tied behind and before with
a piece of leather.   The generality now wear shoes having
only one thin sole."   In 1618 John Taylor says that
" they wore shoes with but one sole a-piece, and stockings
which they call short hose, made of warm stuff of divers
colours, which they call tartans, with blue, flat caps on their
heads."   I fancy that both bonnets and shoes were occasionally worn, but not always.   They were possibly worn by the
gentlemen, but not by the common people.

No mention is made of a sporran, but I think it likely
that one was worn, as there was no pocket in any part of the
old Highland dress.

Martin says that in his time the "trowis" were frequently
worn in the West Highlands.   The dress was introduced from
Ireland in the 16th century.   The main peculiarity of the
costume was that the tight-fitting breeches and the stockings
were united in one garment, which was secured round the
waist by a belt.   These were called long hose, the short hose
were stockings.

All the authorities agree in saying that the dress of the
women, which was called the " arisad " in ancient times, was
very picturesque.   It was designed on the same principle
as the men's.   It consisted of one garment made of white
material, striped with red, black or blue.   It was longer than
the men's, reaching to the ankles.   The lower part, which
was pleated all round, was fastened by a leather belt.   The
upper part was draped round the body.   Red sleeves of
scarlet cloth were worn, which had on them silver buttons set
with fine stones.   The head-dress was a linen kerchief.   Large
locks of hair hung down in front over their cheeks.   A great
many ornaments were worn ; both necklaces and bracelets are
mentioned by Bishop Leslie.   Martin tells us that on the belt

which fastened the skirt was a piece of plate, curiously engraven, about eight inches long by three broad, the end of which was adorned with fine stones or with pieces of red coral.

Out of doors over this dress a plaid was worn, similar to that of the men. " This was fastened on the breast with a buckle of silver or brass, according to the quality of the wearer. It was broad as an ordinary pewter plate, and curiously engraved with animals and other devices."

" A lesser buckle was worn in the middle of the larger one, about two ounces in weight. It had in the centre a large piece of crystal, or some fine stone, and it was set all round with several finer stones of a lesser size."

There has been much controversy as to whether the clan tartans, as we know them, are really ancient or not. It is certain that Highland gentlemen began to wear plaids of divers colours over the lenicroich at a very early period, and that, as Martin says, " a great deal of ingenuity was required in sorting the colours so as to be agreeable to the nicest fancy." From these words one might argue that the colours employed were merely matters of individual taste, but a little further on he says—" Every Isle differs from each other in their fancy of making plaids, as to the stripes, or breadths, or colours. This humour is equally different throughout the mainland of the Highlands, in so far that they who have seen those places, are able, at the first view of a man's plaid, to guess the place of his residence."

Martin, I think, cannot mean that Islands which were divided between two or three clans had only one tartan. They must certainly have been divided into districts just as the mainland was.

It will be observed that he does not say that each clan had its own tartan, but that each island had its own distinctive pattern. He was probably thinking of those clans which, like the Macdonalds of Clanranald and the MacLeods, were in possession of several islands or districts. The former owned South Uist, the Small Isles, and great estates in Garmoran ; the latter possessed Harris, a large part of Skye, and Glenelg.

From Martin's words I infer that, while those clans whose territory was in a ring fence had only one tartan, those whose possessions were widely scattered had several tartans, one for each island or district which they owned, so that an observer could not only tell to what clan a man belonged by viewing the plaid which he wore, but, as Martin says, the " place of his residence."

If this was the case, I think that probably these island tartans were modifications of the one worn by the Chief of the Clan, just as the tartans, which were worn by the different branches of the Clan Donald were modifications of the one worn by the Lord of the Isles. This is clearly seen in the coloured plates which appear in Mr Mackay's book on the subject.

Whether this interpretation of Martin's meaning is true or not, I think that his words clearly prove that distinctive tartans were being worn in the 17th century, and the quotation from Bishop Leslie's statement, which is given above, makes it probable that they were in use a hundred years earlier, when the gentlemen of a clan wore mantles over their saffron shirts.

But all this, I think, applies to the gentlemen. It is extremely doubtful whether the rank and file of a clan ever wore tartans at all. Bishop Leslie implies that their mantles were plain, and when we consider the amount of skill and labour involved in weaving tartans, it is unlikely that it would have been possible to supply the whole clan with such plaids.

None of the early writers give any details as to the patterns worn by particular clans, and with this important branch of the question I have not attempted to deal. I have only striven to show that on the evidence before us it is certain that in ancient times distinctive clan and district tartans were worn by our ancestors, at all events by the gentlemen in each clan.

The character and disposition of the West Highlanders have been described in very varying terms by different writers. The author of the early seventeenth century " Historie of

King James the Sixth " gives the following account of them :—
" Trew it is," he writes, " that thir Islandish men are of nature
verie proud, suspicious, avaritious, full of decept and evill
intentionn each aganis his nychtbour, be what way soever
he can circumvin him. Besydis all this, they are sa crewell
in taking of revenge that neither have they regard to person,
age, tyme or caus ; sa are they all sa far addicted to their
owin tyrannical opinions that, in all respects, they exceid in
creweltie the maist barbarous people that ever has bene, sen
the begynning of the warld."

No doubt this account was written by an extremely pre-
judiced Lowlander, who had no first-hand knowledge of the
Islanders at all, and who based his account of them on the
vague, and probably exaggerated stories of Highland bar-
barities which were flying about the Scottish capital. Still,
it is quite possible that there may be some element of truth
in his description of what the people were in the sixteenth
century. The country was at that time in a terrible state,
and it is quite conceivable that, having lived for more than a
century in such an atmosphere of cruelty and revenge, they
may have lost the kindliness and goodness of heart which was
natural to them.

We shall get a far more correct idea of their real character
from the testimony of men who wrote after this dreadful
time had passed away. Martin Martin, writing at the end of
the seventeenth century, gives the following description of the
West Highlanders :—" They are a very sagacious people.
They have a great genius for music and mechanics. There
are many of them who invent tunes. Some are very dexterous in engraving trees, birds, dogs, etc., on bone, horn or
wood, without any other tool than a sharp-pointed knife. They
have a quick vein of poesy, and compose pieces which power-
fully affect the fancy. They are happily ignorant of many
vices that are practised in the learned and polite world. They
have a great respect for their Chiefs, and they conclude grace
after every meal with a petition to God for their welfare."

I am convinced that Martin has faithfully described to us
the true character of the West Highlanders in his time. Not
one word does he say about their being cruel, treacherous, or

revengeful. He describes them as possessing many excellent and attractive qualities, and we, who know and love their descendants at the present day, realise that his account of them continues to be true now.

It cannot be denied that they had their faults. They had an inordinate pride of race, and despised with whole-hearted but ignorant contempt the Sassenachs, whose methods of life were different to their own. They imagined that there was something degrading in the pursuits of trade and commerce, and thought that warfare, hunting, and athletic sports were the only occupations worthy of a man's attention; they disliked strenuous and sustained exertion, and they threw on the shoulders of the weaker sex the manual labour, which, in other countries, was performed by the men.

In his history (Chapter 3), Macaulay describes in the following words this unfortunate trait in their character :—" An observer, who was qualified to judge the people fairly, would have been struck by the spectacle of athletic men basking in the sun, while their aged mothers and tender daughters were reaping the scanty harvest of oats. Nor did the women repine at their hard lot. In their view it was quite fit that a man, specially if he assumed the aristocratic title of " Duine Uasal," and adorned his bonnet with an eagle's feather, should take his ease, except when he was hunting, fighting or marauding, and in their opinion a high-born gentlemen was much more becomingly employed in plundering the land of others than in tilling his own." Macaulay's pictures are often overdrawn, but I think that it is certain that chivalry towards women was not a virtue of the mediaeval Highlanders. These were serious shortcomings, but our forefathers had many good qualities to set against their faults.

They were essentially a manly people. They delighted in such sports as wrestling, throwing the hammer, putting the stone, and tossing the caber. The Chiefs used often to organise great athletic meetings for their clansmen. To these they invited their brother Chiefs to come and bring with them the finest athletes in their clans to compete with the champions of other clans. These meetings were marked features in the lives which our forefathers lived, and immensely stimulated the keenness for athletic sports amongst the clansmen. A young man thought no effort too great if he could but win the honour of representing his clan at such a gathering.

Hunting the deer was another favourite sport. Great gatherings were held for this purpose, primarily for the amusement of the Chief and his friends, or sometimes to afford an opportunity for the discussion of treasonable designs against the King, but large numbers of the humbler classes were employed at these meetings, and took the greatest delight in them.

Hundreds of men were employed to drive all the deer in a vast tract of country to some given point, where the Chief and his guests awaited them. Numbers of deer-hounds were held in leash till the deer appeared. These were then loosed, the deer were attacked with bows and arrows, in later times with arquebuses ; those that the dogs had pulled down, or those which had been wounded by the sportsmen, were dispatched with dirks and daggers, and it often happened that seventy or eighty deer would be killed in a single drive. The venison so obtained was distributed amongst the people in the neighbourhood.

But athletic sports and hunting were tame things in the eyes of our ancestors compared with the great game of war. They loved the joy of battle for its own sake. They were extraordinarily brave, very hardy, capable of bearing the severest privations, and, as they rendered implicit obedience to their Chiefs, extremely well disciplined. Probably they were and are the finest soldiers in the world.

But mingled with the love of sport and war were very different tastes and qualities which raised them far above the level of savage soldiers, or of men who only lived for pleasure and amusement. They had in them a very real love of music, and their music was not the beating of tom-toms practised by savages, but the high-class music of a refined people. I quote some of Skene's remarks on the subject (Scottish Highlanders, page 140) :—" The style of the Highland airs is singular, being chiefly remarkable for its great simplicity, wildness, and pathos of expression. The scale used is different from the ordinary or diatonic scale, and is defective, wanting the fourth and the seventh, but this very defect gives rise to the pleasing simplicity and plaintiveness of the Highland melody, and imparts to their music a character peculiarly adapted to the nature of their poetry."

The scale Skene refers to is called the pentatonic. One can play it on the piano by starting on F sharp and only playing the black notes. Much old Highland music is in this scale, but in some the diatonic scale, or an approach to it, appears to have been used.

Harps and " clarishas " were the instruments used in early days. The strings of the former were made of sinews, those of the latter were made of brass wire. " These strings they strike either with their nails growing long, or with an instrument appointed for that use. They take great pleasure to decke their harps and clarishas with silver and precious stones, and poor ones who cannot attayne hereunto decke them with Chrystall." (Certayne curious matters touching Scotland, 1797, quoted by Skene). An old Highland harp has been preserved in the family of Lude.

On some ancient stones dating from the ninth century, or even earlier, are carved representations of harps exactly similar to the one at Lude ; therefore it is certain that the harp was used in very early days. Two of these stones reveal the fact that a horn was also used at remote periods for purposes of hunting.

The bagpipes came into use at a later time. Dr MacBain says :—" It came to Scotland in the fourteenth century, and reached the Highlands in the sixteenth century." Major (1521) does not mention it among Highland musical instruments, but Buchanan, 50 years later, says " the Highlanders used it for war purposes. They also improved it by adding the big drone Hence the " piob mhor." It is thoroughly non-Gaelic in origin."

A tradition says that Alasdair, who was the Chief at Dunvegan from 1480 to 1547, gave to the MacCrimmons, the famous pipers of his clan, the lands of Boreraig, where they afterwards founded their college. This tradition may possibly imply that there had not been a family of hereditary pipers attached to the clan before Alasdair's time, and in this way supports Dr MacBain's statement. It is certain that, after this time, pipers, as well as harpers, were attached to the household of every ruler of a clan, and occupied positions of great dignity and importance.

Both classes of men were held in great esteem by the Chiefs, and were highly honoured among all classes of the community. In the seventeenth century accounts at Dunvegan, I find entries for the payment, not only of the Chief's own pipers, the MacCrimmons, but of pipers in all the districts into which the estate was divided. Probably these men were not merely placed in the positions they held to play to the people, but also to instruct the most promising young folk among them in the art of music.

Besides the harpers and pipers who belonged to every clan, bands of wandering minstrels used to traverse the country. They found a cordial welcome alike in the castles of the Chiefs, and in the houses of the people, for they ministered to the love of music which was so strong in all classes.

Fortunately, an immense quantity of the music, which was the delight of the people in the old days, has been preserved. The composers never wrote it down. They could not have done so, for it is probable that they did not know their notes, but their music had the stamp of genius on it, and it has lived on in the memories of the people.

Pipers are still maintained in the households of some Highland families, and a band of pipers is attached to every Highland regiment. These men have preserved a rich store of the old music, the pibrochs, the laments, the salatus, the marches, the strathspeys, the reels, and all the varieties of music which the old composers developed. This music is now safe, it is printed in numerous volumes, though, as might be expected in music which has been handed down by memory from generation to generation, it is not easy to be sure which rendering of any given tune may be the one originally intended by the composer.

Vocal music was no less popular than instrumental among the Highlanders. Now, unhappily, the young people no longer learn the old songs from their elders, and for this

reason there was a very great danger that, as the older generation of people died out, these would be forgotten. Fortunately, enthusiastic collectors, who could speak Gaelic, and
who possessed good ears for music, have been hard at work.
They have visited the people in their homes, they have won
their confidence, they have listened to the old songs, they have
taken down both words and tunes, they have arranged
accompaniments, and the songs, like the old pipe music, are
safe for all time. One of the most indefatigable of these
workers was Miss Frances Tolmie, who only passed to her rest
in December 1926. I had the great privilege of knowing her
well in her later years. To Miss Tolmie, Mrs Kennedy Fraser
owes several of the songs included in her invaluable collection.

Careful study of these songs makes one fact clear ; the
people used to sing at their work. There are songs to be sung
when they were spinning, knitting, weaving, " walking the
cloth " and rowing. Perhaps there is no stronger proof than
this that they had a real love of music in their hearts.

The fact that amongst the pipe music which remains
are many reels implies that the people loved dancing. Dance
music could only have been composed to meet a demand for
it, and I think that the dancing, which forms a part of all
Highland meetings, is a survival of the old love of that amusement, which has been to a great extent killed in modern times
by the strict rules of the Church.

Our forefathers took a keen and intelligent interest in
history. At the banquets of the Chiefs the assembled guests
loved to listen to the tales of the bards and sennachies, which,
in the absence of books, were the only records of the past.

Among the humbler classes the " ceilidhs " were a never-
failing source of joy in the long winter evenings, as, indeed,
they still are. At a ceilidh they gathered together in each
other's houses to tell and listen to old traditions. It is a
remarkable fact that, while these old stories, which we so
highly value now, have been completely forgotten by the well-
to-do classes, they have been remembered and handed down
from one generation to another in the homes of the poor. We
may be thankful that so many have been preserved by ardent

enthusiasts, who deserve our warm gratitude as much as those others who have saved the music of the past from oblivion. I know of no more zealous workers in this direction than Miss Tolmie, previously mentioned, and Mr John Mackenzie, the factor at Dunvegan.

But old traditions concerning the history of bygone days were not the only subjects dealt with at the ceilidhs. The people also loved tales of fairies, water-kelpies, gruagachs, witches, and all kinds of supernatural occurrences. Mr John F. Campbell of Islay has published a large collection of these in his " Popular Tales of the West Highlands," and I have been told a great many of them by Mr Mackenzie. A number of these old stories will be found in Chapter X.

Our fathers were great lovers of poetry, and among them were found many composers of excellent verse. Macaulay's words about the genius of Highland poets are worth quoting. " It is probable that at the Highland banquets minstrels, who did not know their letters, sometimes poured forth rhapsodies in which a discerning critic might have found passages such as would have reminded him of the tenderness of Otway, or of the vigour of Dryden."

The works of many West Highland poets are preserved in the book of James MacGregor, Dean of Lismore (1512), and of Duncan Macrae (born about 1635). Among them are poets in all ranks of life. The second Earl of Argyll, his daughter Isabel, and Sir John Stewart of Appin appear side by side with labourers and farm servants among the poets. Ian Lom (1620-1710), Robert Kirk (1641-1693), Lachlan Mackinnon (died about 1734), Murdoch Matheson, John Mackay (1666-1754), Alexander MacDonald, who was the poet of the Forty-five, are a few whose works have come down to us. Dr George Henderson says that " Clan Ranald's Galley," by the last-named poet, is the finest sea-song in any language. Not very many people can read Gaelic poetry, for many, who can speak the language fluently, cannot read it, but those who can invariably speak in the highest terms of its merits.

One of these fortunate people writes of Angus-a-Eneis, a native of Harris, who lived toward the end of the sixteenth century :—" He was renowned for the richness of his imagery and the depth of his thought." Another writes of Mary MacLeod, the most distinguished of all, who was born in 1615, and lived to the great age of 105, as being " the inimitable poetess of the Isles, and the most original of all our poets." Another writer says :—" Her versification is like a mountain stream running over a smooth bed of granite." The date generally given for Mary's birth is 1588. Professor Henderson shows good reason for believing that the date given above is probably the correct one, but it is impossible to be quite certain.

A race must have a strong vein of poesy in its nature which can produce so many bards, famous in their time, even though, owing to the language in which they expressed their thoughts being a sealed book to most of the world, they and their works are alike forgotten except by a few fortunate people.

It is impossible to conceive that a people possessing such musical, artistic, and poetic tastes can have been the monsters of cruelty, hatred, and revenge, described in the history of King James.

It is not easy to ascertain the religious condition of the people in early days. There can be little doudt that their Celtic ancestors, who had been converted to Christianity by Columba, were sincerely attached to their Church, and there is evidence that the organisation of that Church, though great changes took place in the twelfth century, continued on into later times.

It is difficult to form a decisive opinion as to whether or not the Monastic system had been established at an early period on a large scale in the West Highlands. Personally, I think it probable that it had been so established. St Columba's influence was the great vital force in religious matters throughout the Islands. It is certain that he regarded the foundation of monasteries as the best possible means of spreading Christianity, and of maintaining the zeal of his converts. Before he left Ireland he founded monasteries at Derry, Durrow, and at a great many other places. His first act when he arrived at Iona was to found a monastery there, and I think it is more than likely that he pursued the same policy when he set to work to evangelise the Western Isles, and that wherever he and his disciples went they founded a monastery.

There is some evidence that this theory is correct. There were certainly monastic establishments at Applecross, on the mainland, and at Eigg, where the community included fifty-two persons when they were murdered in 617. The ruins which remain at Columcille, in Skye, and at Sgor nam Ban-'naumha (the Skerry of the Holy Women), in Canna, indicate that in early days there were monasteries or nunneries at both places. The Report of the Royal Commission describes the former as "a cashel or monastery," and says of the latter that "the remains may be those of a cashel or monastic settlement of the Celtic type."

It is quite possible that there may have been a monastery at Rodel, in Harris, as, indeed, tradition asserts. Mackenzie says, in his History of the Outer Hebrides, page 519, on what authority I do not know, that St Clement's was the Church of a priory dependent on the Abbey of Holyrood, and that its foundation is variously attributed to MacLeod, of Harris, and to David I., King of Scotland. If it was really a priory dependent on Holyrood, the latter is the more probable assumption, and the splendour of the Church, which, after Iona, is the finest ecclesiastical building in the Hebrides, points in the same direction. Dean Munro, writing in 1549, describes it as "ane monastery with ane steipil, quhile was foundit and biggit by M'Cloyd of Herray." The Report of the Royal Commission says :—"The Dean seems to be using monastery like minster, as equivalent to a church." I incline to the opinion that the Dean meant what he said, and that, though there is no evidence that there was a monastery at Rodel in Culdee days, there really was one there in the Middle Ages.

On the whole, the evidence which indicates that the monastic system was really established throughout the Western Isles in the days of Columba, and that it continued down to the time of the Reformation, appears to be very strong.

The greatest of all the monasteries was St Columba's own foundation at Iona. I have not attempted to give an exhaustive list of all the religious houses in the Western Isles, and there were many others which I have not mentioned. The monks in all these sacred establishments must certainly have exerted a great influence over the people who lived around them.

Side by side with the Monastic system, the parochial system was flourishing. In Skye there were twelve parishes ; the ruins of three or four of the churches remain. In these we find very few signs which indicate the date when they were built. At Trumpan there is a pointed arch which may be of any date between the thirteenth century and the fifteenth, and it is probable that most of the churches are ancient buildings. They are all very small, and none could have accommodated a large congregation.

Besides the parish churches, there were a great many small chapels. None of them are more than 22 feet long. These may have been attached to outlying townships, and they were possibly served by monks from the monasteries. Only a few ruins remain, but it is certain that they were once very numerous, and they indicate that the people felt the need of religious ministrations, and recognised the duty of worshipping God.

There are some indications that this was really the case. The first Lord of the Isles made generous grants to the Church. These may have earned for him the title " the good Lord John," by which he is known in ancient chronicles. He and a great many other Chiefs were buried at Iona, and the desire to lie in holy ground is a sign that religious feeling was to some extent alive in them.

Tradition says that Alexander Macleod of Dunvegan was a sincerely religious man. An entry in the Lord Treasurer's accounts shews that in 1498 he had a chaplain attached to his household. The entry runs as follows :—
"Given to Rory MacAlexander Mak-Cloydis chapellain iiij ellis of Rissolis blak, price of the eln xxxv S, summa vii £1." It is certain that the same Chief built and endowed two churches in Harris, and it is said that, towards the end of his life, he gave over the government of his clan into the hands

of his son, retired into the monastery of Rodel, and spent his closing years in penitence and prayer.

Even in the sixteenth century, when religion was certainly at a very low ebb, there are one or two hints in some of the old stories that it was not altogether dead. When the clan Ranald MacDonalds invaded the MacLeod country, about the year 1580, they found that all the people were worshipping in the church, but they do not seem to have felt any reverence for a sacred building, for they burnt the church and slaughtered the whole congregation.

I am under the impression that the islanders had at that time almost entirely lost all sense of their religion, and the first statute of Iona implies that most of the churches were in ruins, that there were very few clergy, and that those few were treated with the greatest contempt.

Of book learning our fathers knew nothing. Even the Chiefs could not write their names down to the end of the 16th century. There are many documents in existence signed by them, " with my hand led at ye pen of ye notar because I can writ not." But, if they could neither read nor write, they had wonderful memories. By oral tradition they preserved all the records of the past, the epic poems of their bards, the tales which illustrate their daily life, and handed them down to future generations. I think that it was Plato who deplored the invention of writing, because he thought that it had weakened the powers of the human memory, and possibly people who have no knowledge of books may be really no less well educated than others who have all the advantages that learning can give, and may be, as Martin says of our own ancestors, " ignorant of many vices which are practised in the learned and polite world."

Chapter IV.

HOME LIFE.

CULTIVATION OF THE SOIL, LIVE STOCK, CUTTING PEATS,
LIGHT, SPINNING, WEAVING, IMPORTS AND EXPORTS,
SUPPLY OF ARMS, SHIP-BUILDING, MILITARY TRAIN-
ING, HOMES OF THE PEOPLE.

History and tradition describe the great political and
military events which happened in the past, but do not con-
cern themselves with details about the ordinary life which a
people lived, but in many of the old stories, which have come
down to us, there are references which throw light on such
matters. Moreover, we know something concerning the home
life of the West Highlanders in the seventeenth and eighteenth
centuries. Very few changes took place as time rolled by,
and we may safely assume that what was true of them at a
later period was also true in earlier times.

Food, clothing, fuel, light are necessaries of existence,
and the method by which these were supplied, often under
very great difficulties, are as worthy of our attention as the
more striking and more terrible episodes of clan warfare.

Readers of Dean Munro's account of the Western Isles,
published in 1549, might well imagine that there was no difficulty in supplying all the wants even of a large population.
Neither he nor any other of the early writers mention any of
the adverse circumstances which undoubtedly interfered with
the production of all the necessaries of life. They say nothing
about the disastrous wars which had been waged in the islands
for more than a century, and they say nothing about the
climate.

The islands have a climate which is not without its merits.
Under the influence of the Gulf Stream, the winters are generally, though not always, mild, and to its humid character is
due the magnificent colouring in our landscapes, which a dis-

tinguished artist friend of mine, who had travelled in many parts of the world, pronounced to be more splendid than that in any other region on the globe. The nearest approach to it, he said, was in the islands of the Grecian Archipelago. But from the agriculturist's point of view it cannot be considered a very favourable climate. The rainfall is without doubt very high, violent gales of wind are very prevalent, and even the summers are often very wet and stormy.

It is still more remarkable that these writers describe the soil of almost all the islands as being extremely fertile. We, who know the Hebrides well, find it difficult to understand this description. We know that there are fertile patches in most of them, but, when we think of the great ranges of barren, though splendid, mountains which are often bare rock, and of the hills, on the sides of which nothing but rough bent grass will grow, while on their summits great hags of peat extend for miles, we must admit that only one or two of the islands, possibly Islay and Tyree, can be considered really fertile.

It is possible that in the course of centuries the climate may have altered. It is also possible that certain parts of the land may have lost some of their fertility, but I do not think it very likely that either of these changes has occurred, and I conceive that the production of sufficient food to feed the population was often a matter of great difficulty, specially in times of war. But in spite of a poor soil and a wet climate it is certain that great quantities of cereals were grown.

For various reasons it was probably extremely difficult to import grain at that time. Letters written in the eighteenth century indicate that, even then, it was not easy to do so. One letter describes the great difficulty of getting a ship to carry the corn ; another says how badly the grain in a schooner had been injured by salt water ; a third relates the capture of a vessel, laden with meal for use in Skye, by a French privateer.

For this reason it was absolutely necessary to grow what corn was required at home. On many a hill-side now under heather are lazybeds. These show that corn was once grown there, and, though it is probable that some of the land now ultivated was then undrained marshland, lying, as it does, at a low level close to the sea, or on the banks of rivers, it is certain that much more land was under corn in early days than is the case now.

The crops grown were beare, the Hordeum vulgaris, which is still cultivated in the Long Island ; oats, barley, some flax, from which a coarse linen was woven, and some linseed. Of this cake was made for the maintenance of the cattle in winter. I have found no reference to hay or turnips, and I gather that the herds suffered very severely in hard winters from the lack of these sorts of food.

The methods of cultivation employed, even at a much later period, were extremely primitive. The plough in use is thus described in an account of Harris, dated 1772 :—" Its whole length is but four feet seven inches, it is drawn by four horses abreast, it has one handle by which it is directed. The mould board is fastened with two leather thongs, and the soke and coulter are bound together at the point by a ring of iron." " Another instrument is also used, called a ristle. It is only two feet long, and is drawn by one horse. It has no soke, but has a sharp crooked coulter. This is drawn through the soil near ten inches deep. The use of it is to be drawn before the plough in order to cut the long, twisted roots of a number of plants with which the sandy soil of Harris is infested. These are powerful enough to obstruct the progress of so weak a plough as that which is commonly used." Much of the cultivation was done with the " caschrom," the old kind of spade then in use. Dean Monro, writing in 1549 about Harris, says that " twisse mair of delving is done in it nor of tilling." This means that two-thirds of the soil were dug with the spade, not ploughed. In spite of all the efforts made by the people to grow sufficient corn for their own requirements, they were occasionally very short of meal. Then, as now, the crops sometimes failed, but the seannachies say that in such years they did manage somehow to import some grain.

There were great numbers of live stock in the country. One of my correspondents speaks of pigs, but I think that the Highlanders did not keep this kind of animal. But they certainly possessed large flocks of sheep, probably of a breed similar to that still found in St Kilda, very small, but very

hardy, and thoroughly suited to the climate of the West Highlands. Bishop Leslie gives a most remarkable description
of the St Kilda sheep. The old name of St Kilda is Hirth.
" Hirth has its name from a certaine scheip quhilkis in thir
only island did abound. The scheip may be comparit in height
to a gait, and in greatness to a buffel (a buffalo). Thair
hornis in length exceid those of a buffel." He goes on to
describe the sheep still to be found on Soa as " very wilde
scheip, whether to call thame scheip or gait I know not, they
have neither wool like a scheip nor hair like a gait." In 1542
a sheep was worth two pence.

The old rent rolls show, from the number of hens paid in
lieu of money, that a great deal of poultry was then kept,
and it is probable that this was also the case in earlier times.
In 1542 the price of hens was six for a penny.

The letterpress on the back of a map of Skye, published
in 1650, tells us that there were at that time great
droves of semi-wild horses wandering about the country.
These were probably rather ponies than horses, but of a strong
and serviceable breed. A great many of these would be required for the method of cultivation described above, and I
am under the impression that the Highlanders in old days
did a great deal more riding on horseback than their descendants do now.

The black cattle were the main wealth of the Highlands
up to the end of the 18th century. These were most extraordinarily hardy animals, capable of bearing any amount of
exposure to the weather, and extremely picturesque. They
supplied the milk, butter and cheese which formed so impor-
ant a part of the food consumed by the people; from their
hides the leather was prepared of which the clansmen made
their shoes, and from the herds were taken the marts, as the
beasts were called which were killed every autumn, and
salted down for food in the winter.

During the bad times, when the clan feuds were raging, cattle
were constantly being carried off by hostile marauders ; and
some of the most thrilling stories of clan warfare relate how
the raiders collected great numbers of cattle, and how, their
retreat being necessarily slow, they were overtaken, and

desperate battles fought for the recovery of the spoil. One wonders how any herds remained when this was constantly going on.

One feature of life in the old days was the annual migration to the Sheillings, the equivalent of the Norwegian Saeters. Every summer the cattle were sent up to the hills, in charge of women and girls, to utilise the grass on the high ground, and a busy summer was spent tending the herds, making cheese, and churning butter. The scene of many of the old legends is laid in the sheillings.

All the operations on a West Highland farm involved an enormous amount of labour. One very remarkable circumstance clearly appears in some of the old stories. From these it seems that there were absolutely no fences of any kind in the country. It was not till towards the end of the 18th century that the importance of building fences round the steadings and arable fields began to be realised. All the old walls and dykes, of which there are so many now in the country, were put up about that period. The result of this was that, as there were no fences round any of the fields on which cereals were grown, from the time when the young corn appeared above the ground to the day on which the harvest was carried, the fields had to be watched day and night to prevent the herds from doing harm to the crops.

The corn was ground in hand-mills or querns. Pennant says it was a very labourious process, and that it took two women four hours to grind a bushel of corn. There were no mills in Skye until about 1730. He also describes a method of burning the corn, called the " graddan," which took the place of threshing. " This is performed in two ways, first by cutting off the ears and drying them in a kiln, then setting fire to them on a floor, and picking out the grain, by this operation rendered as black as coal. The second method is more expeditious, but very wasteful, as it destroys both thatch and manure. In this the whole sheaf is burnt without cutting off the heads."

Herding the cattle, taking them up to the sheillings in summer, milking the cows morning and evening, churning the butter and making the cheese required constant and unremitting attention. The sheep probably took care of themselves during most of the year, but, in the lambing season, it was necessary to protect the lambs from foxes, of which there were great numbers ; from eagles, which were fairly numerous, and from ravens, which abounded. Plucking the wool off the backs of the sheep, which was the practice instead of the more modern method of clipping, took a long time, and involved much toil.

Besides all this, the peats had to be cut, dried, stacked, and carried home. A householder in the South, who orders a ton of coal, and has it delivered and put in his cellar, without any further trouble on his part, will find it difficult to realise the amount of labour which is even now expended by the Highlanders in securing the supply of fuel they require. Sometimes this labour is all in vain, for, in a very wet year, it may be impossible to dry the peats. This actually happened in 1923. In such years the people must have had to endure great hardships in the winter. Possibly the birchwoods, of which there were many more then than now, were cut down for firewood when the peats failed. The same fuel was used in the forges of the blacksmiths. Mr Mackenzie writes as follows on the subject :—

" In the smithies peats were the only fuel used, but this had to be converted into a sort of charcoal—which I have seen myself done—and the old blacksmith used to say that its heat was greater than that of any coal, but that the trouble of converting it into charcoal was considerable, and that a good deal of the peat was wasted. Yet, when labour was cheap, the conversion would present no great difficulty. I know of one place from which peat was taken for conversion into charcoal. Every kind of peat won't do, and the conversion must be from the black peat, which is usually found at a depth of ' four peats.' "

The supply of light, which was so urgently required in the long winter evenings, was always a difficulty. In parts of the Highlands, where pines grew freely, resin was extracted from these, and burnt in receptacles called " pyrnies," but in the islands there were no pine woods. Here seals were killed in large numbers, and oil extracted from their carcases. In

St Kilda this was obtained from the fulmar petrels, which breed in such numbers on the island. The lamp which, it is said, Lady Grange used during her detention at St Kilda, is preserved at Dunvegan. It is a low iron receptacle, rather like a flat cream jug, with a very long, upright handle. In this oil was placed, and a wick, floating upon it, gave a most miserable light.

It is certain that in later times the Highlanders used tallow candles, made at home from the fat of animals, but I have not been able to ascertain when they began to do this. The processes used in the making of clothes were very laborious. The materials used were wool and linen, which were spun on the old-fashioned spindle and distaff. The spinning-wheel did not come into use until about 1750.

The distaff was a bar of wood, to which the material to be spun was loosely attached, generally by being wrapped up in a soft ball, into which the end of the distaff was inserted. The spindle was a smaller tapering piece of wood, with a weight of stone or earthenware at the bottom, and a slit to take the thread at the top. The distaff was held under the left arm of the spinner, the spindle was made to rotate and recede from the spinner by a dexterous twist, the thread being drawn out between the fore-finger and the thumb of the right hand so long as the twisting of the spindle lasted. It was then drawn in, new material put on it, and the operation was repeated.

When the wool or linen was spun, it was dyed with colours from plants, which had to be searched for on the hills ; it was then woven in hand-looms.

Not only was the cloth of one colour so woven, but tartans with elaborate patterns. " The plaid," says Martin, " is made of fine wool, it consists of divers colours, and there is a great deal of ingenuity required in sorting the colours, so as to be agreeable to the nicest fancy. For this reason the women are at great pains to give an exact pattern of the plaid upon a piece of wood, having the numbers of every thread of the stripe upon it."

When the weaving was finished, the cloth had to be fulled and cleansed from oil and grease, and this was done by what was called the "Laughad," or "walking" the cloth.

Pennant describes the operation in the following words :—
" Twelve or fourteen women sit down on each side of a long
board, ribbed lengthways, putting the cloth upon it. First
they work it backwards and forwards with their hands, and
they then use their feet, singing all the time with such fury
that you might imagine a troop of female demoniacs to have
been assembled."

Another industry was the tanning of leather made from
the skins of animals, and, when the cloth and leather were
prepared, the work of making cloths and shoes was all carried
out at home.

All this implies that each of the West Highland clans
was, to some extent, a self-sufficing community ; the needs of
which were supplied by the produce of its own country, and
by the labours of its own clansmen. The barley oats and
beare which they required were grown in their own fields, and
ground in their own querns by their own toil ; the butter,
cheese and meat which they consumed were the produce of
their own flocks and herds. The great beds of peat supplied
them with fuel, which they cut, dried, stacked and carried
home by their own labour. They made their own linen from
home-grown flax ; they spun the wool which their own sheep
produced ; they dyed it with dyes of varied colours, which
were derived from plants which grew wild on the hills. From
the wool they knitted their own stockings, and wove cloth of
singular excellence and beauty. They made their own
clothes with the cloth, and their own shoes with leather prepared by themselves from the skins of their own animals.
The black huts in which they lived were built by their own
hands.

But they were not quite self-sufficing ; there were
some articles which it was absolutely necessary to import.
Even if the arms and armour were all made at home, as there
was no iron in the country, the raw material must have been
imported, and it seems probable that corn, wine and brandy
were also brought from abroad.

That means that there was certainly some trade between
the West Highlands and other parts of the world, possibly,
it has been suggested, with France, the Mediterranean ports,

the low countries, the Baltic, and the South of Scotland. Probably adventurous ship masters from all these places paid occasional visits to the Western Isles. It is possible that strings of pack horses might have brought merchandise to some points on the mainland, from which it could be shipped to the islands, and that droves of cattle might have been driven to the markets in the South ; but I think it more likely that whatever trade there may have been was sea-borne, specially when we consider how often the country, through which the pack-horses and the cattle would have to pass, was in a condition of frightful disturbance.

And what were the exports ? In an extract from his will, King Robert Bruce mentions cattle, but from the Outer Islands they must go part of the way by sea, and it would not have been easy to stow much live stock in the ships of the period. Possibly by cattle the King meant salted carcases. Nothing but salt meat was consumed in Scotland during the winter up to a much later date, and the demand for this article of food must have been very great. Some cheese and butter, some hides, some wool and cloth, and a few sheep may be included in the list. If, as I think, the internal condition of the Islands was peaceful during these early centuries, there was probably a great deal of surplus produce available for export.

There were, and are, great numbers of sea birds, including eider ducks, on our shores. Feathers are still exported from St Kilda, and it is quite likely that there was a demand for them in old days. Indubitably hawking was a favourite form of sport, and large numbers of falcons were needed. James IV., in a charter to MacLeod, dated 1498, reserved the eyries or falcons' nests. Dundee, in a letter to MacLeod in 1689, asks as a great favour for one of his falcons. It is quite likely that a good many of these birds, which breed in the rocks of our islands, were sent South. There they commanded high prices.

Hector Boece, writing in 1526, says that in the Loch Ness district " ar many martrikis (martens), bevers, quhitredis (weasels) and toddis (foxes). The furrings and skinnis of thaim are coft (bought) at gret price among uncouth mer-

chandise." If there was " uncouth merchandise " in furs at
Inverness, there may also have been a similar trade in the
Islands. I have read that beavers formerly existed in Wales,
but I have never heard that any were found in Scotland. Still,
it is quite possible that there may have been some of these
animals at one time in the Islands, and that, their skins being
so valuable, they were killed down. There are plenty of the
other animals mentioned at the present day in the Western
Isles.

One would expect to find large quantities of salt fish among
the exports. All the world was then Roman Catholic ; Lent
and other fast-days were rigorously observed, and the demand
for fish must have been enormous. No country in the world
could better have supplied this demand. The sea which
surrounded the islands teemed with fish of all kinds ; the
Islanders lived on its shores ; they possessed boats, there was
nothing to prevent them catching any quantity of fish, but
all the evidence we have points to their having done very
little in this direction.

In only one old story, out of the many with which I am
acquainted, is fishing referred to. In a report on the Islands,
dated 1590, the author again and again refers to the vast
quantities of fish in Hebridean waters, and constantly repeats
the remark—" The people mak na labour as to slaying any
fisches." Captain Dymes, in 1636, in his description of
Lewis, says :—" The great and rich commodity which might
be made of this land is the fishinge, whereof the inhabitants
do make but small benefit besides their own food . . .
they are so far from having the true industry of killing cod
and ling, that one boat with our Newfoundland men will kill
more fish in a day than they with one of their boats will kill
in a year." Fish were so plentiful, he goes on, that " four
Dutch busses in three months made £7500 clear gain." A
hundred and fifty years later the report on Harris in 1772
says the same thing. Pennant, describing the disastrous
famine in the same year, says " the people were reduced to
picking up shell-fish on the sea shore," but not one word does
he say about any attempt being made to reap the plenteous
harvest of the sea. The only conclusion we can arrive at on

all this evidence is that very little fishing was done by the West Highlanders in early days.

My friend, Mr Mackenzie, takes a different view, and his opinion is certainly worthy of respect. I quote from a letter he wrote in answer to one of mine—

" At the present moment I cannot bring forward much evidence against the views expressed by Skene and the others you mention regarding the fishings in our country either for home consumption or export, but I know it to be the local tradition that fish (with which I include shell-fish) formed a considerable portion of the food of the people."

" Dean Munro, when travelling through the islands of his Deanery in 1549, mentions fishings as being good in many of the islands. Of Skye he writes :—

" Into thir ile there is three principal salt water loches, to wit, Loche Sleigachan, Loche Downort, and Loche Sleipan. In thir three principal loches there is a guid take of herrings ; for-by thir three principal loches, also within this ile, to wit 1 Loche Skahanask, 2 Loche Emorte, 3 Loche Vrakdill, 4 Loche Kensale serloss, 5 Loche Dunbegan, 6 Loche Gorsarmis, 7 Loche Annoscort, 8 Loche Snasporte, 9 Loche Portri, 10 Loche Ken, 11 Loche Nadale in Sleit. The uther twa Loches my memory has fayled of them ; but in mony of them there is guid tack of herrings sometymes, but naught so guid by far as in the first three loches."

" Practically all the inhabited islands yielded fish in considerable quantities. Of Harris he says :—" It is very fertile and fruitful for corne, store, and fischings."

" Seeing that Dean Munro was a century before Martin, it goes to a certain extent to prove that in ancient times considerable fisheries did exist.

" Should I come across anything further which might throw greater light on export I will at once let you know. If fish was an article of trade to the Continent and Mediterranean, there must have been an import of salt to enable the people to cure the fish. The difficulty of getting salt may account for the neglect of the fishing industry."

Such were the peaceful labours of the people. Their recreations and amusements I have dealt with in Chapter III. But one all-absorbing occupation of the men remains to be described. Considering that in those days the clans were constantly engaged in warfare, either external or internal, the maintenance of military efficiency must have been one of the first matters to be dealt with, even when the land was at peace.

The means of destroying life were as important as the means of sustaining life, and the very existence of a clan depended on the possession of sufficient arms and armour to equip its men. The supply was, I imagine, the most difficult problem which a mediaeval Chief had to solve. A clan was frequently prevented from putting its whole available force into the field by the lack of these necessaries. The clansmen used a great variety of weapons when they went out to battle.

Up to the end of the sixteenth century fire-arms were not used. Darts or javelins were " thrown with great force and skill," and one division of a Highland army always consisted of archers. Boswell mentions that, when he visited Dunvegan, the bow of Sir Rory MacLeod was still preserved there, and adds that " hardly any man now can bend it."

For fighting at close quarters the clansmen were armed with broad two-handed swords (the weapon preserved at Dunvegan is one of them), with battle-axes, and with dirks, which were only sharpened on one side.

The supply of these offensive weapons for a large force must have been a serious matter, but there were even greater difficulties to be overcome. All the authorities speak of defensive armour being worn. It is thus described—" An iron bonnet, and an habergeon or shirt of mail made of iron links, so long that it reached to their heels." At Dunvegan, several coats of such mail and one or two iron bonnets are preserved, and I think it is certain that the Chiefs and some of the leading men of each clan wore armour.

In the report, from which I have already made some quotations, it is stated that a third of the clansmen wore defensive armour, but I very much doubt the possibility of providing coats of mail for so large a proportion of the men. In an old tradition which describes one of the fights between two clans, it is related that on each side was a smith clad in complete armour, probably made by themselves, and that they fought a sort of duel while their companions looked on. This seems to imply that they were the only two who wore defensive armour. Moreover, the frightful losses suffered on both sides in some of the clan battles induce me to think that only a few wore coats of mail. In the contemporary wars in Italy the mercenaries, equipped cap-a-pie in plate armour, often fought for a whole day without any serious casualties at all taking place. The terrible losses endured by the Highlanders were probably due to lack of defensive armour.

Some seannachies believed that the weapons and armour were imported from abroad. Others maintained that they were made at home. I have been able to find no evidence that an hereditary armourer was attached to the household of any Chief, and it is doubtful whether, if the word is used in its strict sense, there were any armourers at all in the country, but there were certainly a good many blacksmiths, and it is probable that they made, at all events, some of the arms and armour which were so urgently needed.

It must also be remembered that each of the Island clans was not only a military power, but a naval power, and had its fleet of birlinns or galleys. Such a vessel, with " sailing geir compleit " and 26 oars, was part of the dowry given by Sir Rory MacLeod of Dunvegan with his daughter Moir, on her marriage to young Clan Ranald in 1613.

Therefore, there can be no doubt that a very important ship-building industry was being carried on in the country. The MacNeills of Barra had the reputation of being the best builders of birlinns in the West Highlands.

There was wood on the mainland, which was used in building houses, and there may have been timber there which was suitable for ship-bullding, but in the islands there were no trees, except low-stunted birch. And this certainly could not be used for such a purpose.

Unfortunately, we have no knowledge as to what a birlinn or galley was like. As far as I know, not one has been preserved, neither are there any old prints or pictures of them. I conjecture that they resembled the dragon ships of the Norsemen.

A report to the English Privy Council in 1545 describes the arrival of 4000 Islanders to co-operate with the troops of Henry VIII. in Ireland. In this it is stated that 1000 of them were "tall marryners for rowing of the galleys." Gregory says in his history (page 170) that the fleet which conveyed these men to Ireland consisted of 180 galleys. From this I gather that each galley carried about 22 men on an average, but it is probable that some were larger, and that others were much smaller. Some, we know, were propelled by 26 oars, and in one case a galley with 36 oars is mentioned.

The training of the manhood of the clan in the art of war was no less important than the supply of arms and ships. No man wearing a heavy suit of mail could be capable of strenuous and prolonged exertion unless he had been accustomed to bear its weight from his youth. The gentlemen who tried to revive an old-day tournament at Eglinton in the last century discovered this. Their lack of skill in wearing their armour and using their weapons was one of the reasons why what should have been a brilliant pageant was something of a fiasco.

No man can be an efficient archer until he has perfected himself in the art of shooting with the bow by long and patient practice, as the famous bowmen of England well knew. No man can wield a sword with effect till he has learnt all that a fencing school can teach, or a battle-axe till he understands his weapon ; no man can defend himself with his targe till he has learnt how to use it.

Though the severe course of drill in a barrack yard, which is essential in the making of a soldier in the regular army, was not necessary for the Highlanders, they had to be trained in their own peculiar methods of fighting. Even the desperate charges, which so often in later days broke the ranks of the hardiest veterans, and which seemed so spontaneous, had been rehearsed a hundred times while the preparation for war was going on in peaceful days.

Therefore, the most important employment of the clansmen, when the land was at rest, was the incessant training, which alone could make them efficient when war broke out. Probably this strenuous education in the art of war was even more marked in the households of the Chiefs than anywhere else. Tradition tells us how one Chief, who had been severely wounded at Harlaw, and incapacitated from active service in the field, spent his enforced leisure. He was one of the finest swordsmen of his day, and during the rest of his life it was his daily delight to fence with the members of his household, and teach them how to use their swords to the best effect.

Another Chief lived to be nearly a hundred years old. The training of his youthful kinsmen in the art of war was the main employment of his old age, and he used to give suits of armour as prizes to those who acquitted themselves best.

The houses in which the people lived are no less interesting than the lives they led. In the Western Isles are many earth houses ; there are also many brochs and duns, but I do not propose to deal with them, interesting as they are from an antiquarian point of view. After them, the oldest edifices in the country are the castles, the homes of the Chiefs. Of these there are a great many on our shores. As far as I know, only two are still inhabited, Duart and Dunvegan ; the rest are all of them in ruins. It is quite clear that the one thought in the minds of the men who built these strongholds was security. Sites of great natural strength were chosen. One or two stand on rocky islets surrounded by the sea. MacNeill's Fortress in Barra is one of these, and Eilan Donan is on an islet at high tide. Others, like Dunvegan and Dunskaith, stand on isolated rocks. But most of them are situated at the end of promontories. They are protected on three sides by precipices, which rise abruptly out of the sea, and all are built on rocks above sheltered bays, where the fleets of galleys belonging to their owners could lie securely at anchor.

This is alone enough to show that they were built by a seafaring people. These naturally strong positions were further strengthened by every device which the mind of man could conceive. The gateway was narrow, the iron-studded door was massive and of great strength, while holes in the masonry behind the door show where huge bars, probably of iron, made it yet more difficult to force an entrance. Behind the door was the portcullis, which rose and fell in grooves, which can still be seen. When he had forced the gate, an enemy would find himself in a narrow passage, which two or three resolute men, clad in armour, could hold against an army, and where he would be harassed by the missiles which the defenders could fling upon his head from above. At Dunskaith this passage took the form of a steep stair, with several turns in it. On this a desperate defence could be put up.

When all these difficulties were overcome, the enemy was only in the baillie, and he still had to force his way into the keep, and this was enormously strong. The walls at Dunvegan are nine feet thick, and nothing but modern artillery could batter them down. The windows were mere slits in the wall, through which not even a boy could creep. These castles were practically impregnable ; nothing but starvation could force their garrisons to surrender, and there are very few records, if, indeed, there are any, of one of them being captured.

One remarkable circumstance about all these West Highland castles is that they are very small. Ardtornish, once the principal seat of the Island Lords, consists of a single keep, 72 feet by 51½ ; Dunvegan, until the end of the fifteenth century, also only contained a single keep, about 55 feet by 40 feet, and most of the castles are much smaller. How in such buildings could a Chief keep up the state I have described ? It is at least possible that there were attached to each of these keeps less solid structures, which have disappeared. When a building is in ruins, people very often take the old stones to save themselves the expense and trouble of quarrying and dressing fresh ones, and in this way extensive ranges of building may have entirely disappeared. Moreover, till one has excavated round an old castle, one can never be sure that mounds, which look natural, may not be really due to fallen masonry which lies below them.   It is therefore quite reasonable to suppose that these old castles were once much larger than they now seem to have been.   There is one circumstance at Dunvegan which lends some probability to this theory.   The keep is at the north end of the rock.   About 1490 another tower was built at the south end of the rock. Why was it not built beside the keep ?   The reason may be that there was then a range of buildings there, and that this was taken down when a new wing was built on the site early in the seventeenth century.

A question of great interest arises : When were these old castles built ?   The generally received theory is that there were no stone castles in the Western Isles before the thirteenth century.   I do not think that that theory can be maintained. Indeed, it is not in accordance with facts.   The brochs and duns, though they differ in shape and method of construction from the castellated buildings we are considering, are stone castles, and it is not correct to say that none such exist in a country where they abound.

But, apart from this, is the theory reasonable ?   The Norsemen, who were settling in the Western Isles in the ninth and following centuries, were living amongst a con-quered population, who might rise against them at any moment ; and they were exposed to the raids of pirates, who were none the less to be feared because they were Norse-men like themselves.   For these reasons I think that it is certain that the Norsemen must have required and built fortresses of some kind.

It has been suggested that they built them of wood, and that for this reason all trace of them has disappeared.   But when we remember that there was no wood suitable for building purposes in the islands, and that they would have been obliged to bring it from the mainland by sea, this seems to be a most improbable theory.   It is, in my opinion, far more likely that they built their strongholds of stone, of which there was any quantity close at hand, and if they really did this, the ruins of their castles would remain.

Surely then when we find numerous castles of unknown antiquity in the Western Isles, it is not an unreasonable hypothesis that some of them were built by the Norse-men during the ninth and following centuries. Some may have been built from the foundations at a much later date ; some may have been altered and remodelled in subsequent years. But I firmly believe that many of the castles were originally built by the Norsemen, and that some of them may be as early as the end of the ninth century.

That is the date which tradition assigns to the oldest part of Dunvegan, and the architectural evidence which re-mains convinces me that the tradition is not very far wrong. Kismul Castle in Barra is another building of the most venerable antiquity. In both these buildings the stair-cases which lead to the roof, unlike those in southern castles, are straight flights of stairs ascending in the thickness of the walls, and turning at the angles. In both the masonry is random rubble, which was only employed in important build-ings at an early date ; in both the windows are very small, and absolutely plain, which was unusual in Norman castles, and the sea gate at Dunvegan, where the voussoirs in the arch are rough and jagged, numerous and long, with very wide joints between them, must clearly date from a very early period, quite possibly from the ninth century.

Every Chief in old days possessed his castle, and it was the centre round which revolved the life of his clan. There he held his court, surrounded by his household, his harpers, his pipers, his bards, his jesters, and his guards. There were gathered the gentlemen in attendance and their retainers. There day by day came clansmen to ask for favours, or to lodge complaints. There came the Chiefs of neighbouring clans to discuss some weighty matter of Island politics, to take part in some great hunting or athletic meeting, or to enjoy the pleasures of social intercourse.

Two accounts have come down to us of the splendid hospitality of Dunvegan in the old days. About the year 1620, a Bard of Clanranald's describes a house party, as we should call it, which lasted several days, and seems to have been an orgy of eating and drinking (see a note in Scott's Lord of the Isles). Mary MacLeod, the famous poetess, tells us of another far pleasanter gathering, which probably took place about 1670. The great house is filled with guests, and all are gathered together in the banqueting hall. Some of the older guests are playing chess, others are seated at a table, drinking wine out of horn goblets. Among them is " Sir Norman of the Banners," Mary's favourite hero, " unsurpassed for the manliness of his form and the readiness of his wit." Young men and maidens throng the hall, and are full of merriment and mirth. When the guests are tired of amusing themselves, the seannachies and bards recite some moving legend of the past, or harpers pour forth floods of entrancing melody, and so the time flies all too quickly by. I do not doubt that in the castles of other chiefs the same kindly hospitality was offered to all who chose to avail themselves of it.

When a chief had several castles on his estate, he sometimes appointed some of his more important chieftains to be constables of these castles. The Macraes were constables of Eilan Donan, the Campbells of Dunstafnage were constables of that castle, and tradition says the MacCaskills were constables of Dunskaith. So some of the chieftains were well housed, but most of them lived in poor abodes. At a time when on any day an enemy might raid the country, and reduce all the houses in it to ashes, it was worth no man's while to build a dwelling which could not be repaired by a very small amount of labour. Possibly, before the clan feuds began, they may have lived in better houses ; they certainly did at a later period, but up to the latter part of the 18th century their homes were little more than hovels.

The masses of the people dwelt in black huts, built by themselves, which some of us, who knew the Highlands forty or fifty years ago, can remember so well, but which have in many parts of the country become almost entirely disused. Mr Colin Sinclair gives the following description of this type of dwelling-house :—

"The cottage of the peasant consisted of four walls and a roof, forming a building of rectangular plan. The walls were usually constructed of rubble stones, laid without mortar, and of considerable thickness—varying from three feet to even six feet. In the latter case the wall was often formed of two sections in thickness, with a hollow space between, commonly filled up solidly with moss and earth. The house often consisted of but one room, but frequently a cross partition of wattles and clay was introduced, dividing the house into a larger and a smaller apartment. The fire was placed in the middle of the floor of the larger apartment, which was used as the general living room, while the smaller was reserved for the live stock.

" In the construction of the roof, couples of round timber were placed at wide intervals across the building. Over the couple timbers, longitudinal *purlins* were placed, supporting the bed-work of wattles and turf upon which the thatch was laid. The thatch consisted of turf, heath or rushes. The roofs were usually constructed with hip ends, the four walls being of equal height, without gables. This form is characteristic of the most rudimentary manner of roof construction, finding its prototype in the " bee-hive " structure as exemplified in the huts of primitive peoples, the gable-end type being a somewhat later development, pertaining more to the mainland than to the islands. The pitch of the roofs was considerably less than forty-five degrees, thereby dispensing with much timber, a scarce commodity in the islands, and at the same time minimising the effect of wind pressure. In many of the island dwellings the general surface of the roof springs from a point towards the inside face of the walls, the thatch being kept well back from the outer edge. Thus in walls of such thickness as were employed, a flat ledge of wall-top remained uncovered. This arrangement is to be found in many localities among the islands at the present day. The house usually had but one door, and often no windows. Directly over the fire an aperture was formed in the roof, through which part of the smoke escaped, the remainder filling the house and finding its way out by the door."

When one entered such a house one's first impression was that it was a terribly comfortless abode ; it was very small, very dark, and the upper part of the room so full of peat smoke that one could see scarcely anything till one sat down. When we compare these old dwellings with those in which the crofters now live, we are apt to think that the change from the one to the other kind of house is the greatest improvement which has taken place in recent years. I am not quite sure ; there is something to be said for this type of house. The hole in the roof, through which the smoke escaped, ventilated the dwelling, and this was no small advantage. A medical friend was telling me some time ago about the alarming increase of tuberculosis in the Highlands. I asked him what he thought was the reason. He answered, " The passing away of the black hut." Probably in these humble homes of the poor there was much pleasant social intercourse. In them ceilidhs were held, many tales were told, many songs were sung, possibly some one would be present who could play the harp or the bagpipes, and the evenings were as cheerful and happy as those which the Chief and his guests spent in the castle.

Chapter V.

INTERNAL AND EXTERNAL WARFARE.

CESSION OF ISLES BY NORWAY TO SCOTLAND—THE LORD-
SHIP OF THE ISLES—INTERNAL WARS BEFORE 1266—
EXTERNAL WARS IN 13th, 14th, 15th, AND 16th CEN-
TURIES—INTERNAL WARS IN 15th AND 16th CEN-
TURIES—CONDITION OF THE COUNTRY—WARS ON
BEHALF OF THE STUART KINGS.

Up to 1266, while the Norse Kings still ruled in Man and
the Isles, the Islands were the scene of much internal warfare.
In 1158, Somerled reduced the Kingdom of Man to the verge
of ruin.   In 1230 (says the Saga of King Haakon) there was
great " unrest in the Syderies," due to the efforts of Olaf the
Black to regain his rightful inheritance.   In the same Saga
we are told that in the summer of 1262, Haakon received a
letter from the King of Man.   This informed him that the
Scots had invaded Skye, burnt houses and churches there,
killed men and women, and spitted little children on their
spears.   It was this letter which caused Haakon to decide
on his own invasion of Scotland, which took place in 1263.

After the fall of the Norse Kingdom, the Western Clans
were constantly at war, but it was no longer internal warfare, it was external warfare waged in parts of Scotland far
removed from the Western Isles.   This was certainly the
case at the end of the thirteenth century.

We are apt to imagine that Robert Bruce won the Crown
at Bannockburn, and we forget that during many years he
was engaged in a desperate struggle, in the course of which
scores of battles and skirmishes were fought with varying
success.   It is more than probable that men from the Hebrides
were engaged in all of these ; it is certain that many of them
had their share in the crowning victory of Bannockburn.
John Major, a 16th century writer, says " That great-souled
King, Robert Bruce, gives this counsel in his last will and

testament, that the Kings should never part themselves from these Islands, inasmuch as they could thence have cattle in plenty, and stout warriors." These words shew how warmly the King appreciated the help which the Islanders had given.

The history of Scotland during the remainder of the fourteenth century is one long record of desperate battles. Dupplin, Halidon Hill, Neville's Cross are only three out of the many that might be named.

At this time each of the Island Chiefs was a vassal of one or other of the four mesne Lords amongst whom the Western Isles were then divided. All of these Barons were taking part in the wars to which I have referred. It is certain that, when they were themselves engaged in warfare, they summoned their vassals to join the array of their Baronies, and fight under their banners, and, I think, it is no less certain that, since they possessed ample power to enforce their commands, their orders were obeyed. It is true that the old chroniclers never mention the names of particular clans which were engaged in the battles they describe, probably because they regarded even the most powerful clans as no more than units in the array of their superior Lord.

As time went on, by a remarkable series of accidents, the four Baronies which Alexander III. had created were united into one, and the Islay Chief became Lord of the Isles. After the triumph of Robert Bruce, John de Ergadia, who had been one of the bitterest enemies of the King, was forfeited, and his estates were divided between Angus of Islay and Allan MacRuari. A little later the latter was killed in a quarrel with the Earl of Ross. He left no male heir, his sister Amy became his heiress, and brought all her estates to her husband, the " good Lord John of Islay." It was then that the latter assumed the proud title of Dominus Insularum, and became the first Lord of the Isles.

In his son's time some of the clans, notably the MacLeods, refused to acknowledge the authority of the Island Lord, and between 1390 and 1400 some desperate fighting took place between him and these recalcitrant clans, but, by the beginning of the 15th century, by persuasion or force, all the Island Chiefs had been brought to accept him as their superior Lord, and he was practically an independent sovereign for nearly a hundred years. Although some of the clans had unwillingly acknowledged the Island Lord as their superior, as time went on the successive Lords of the Isles earned the whole-hearted affection and devotion of their vassals, and probably the period during which they ruled over the Islands was a golden age in West Highland history.

The relations between the Island Lords and the Chiefs should be studied. Each of them, though he acknowledged the Island Lord as his superior, and followed him in his wars, remained the absolute ruler of all the people who lived in his own country. The Island Lordship was a confederacy, made up of a number of semi-independent clans, under a head who never acted without the advice of his Council. This Council consisted of seventeen Chiefs, who met at first in Islay, afterwards in Eigg, to settle such great questions as peace and war, and to deal with all matters, external and internal, in which the interests of the Lordship as a whole were involved.

It is possible that the Lordship of the Isles at different times may have included a larger or a smaller number of clans, and, when its Lord was also Earl of Ross, the mainland Chiefs in that Earldom owed him obedience, but seventeen was the number of Chiefs who in 1545 entered into negotiations with Henry VIII., and swore allegiance to him. These are named in a State paper published by Tytler, and given in Gregory's history, page 170. Besides Donald Dubh, who claimed to be Lord of the Isles, were

Hector Maclean of Doward.
Murdoch MacLean of Loch Buy.
Allan MacLean of Torlusk
John MacLean of Coll.
John MacLean of Ardgour.
Donald MacLean of Kengarloch.
John MacQuarrie of Ulva.
John MacAllaster, Captain of Clan Ranald.
Angus MacDonald, brother german of James Macdonald.
Archibald MacDonald of Sleat.

Alexander MacIan of Ardnamurchan.
Angus Ranaldson of Knoydert.
Alexander Ranaldson MacDonald of Glengarry.
Rorie MacLeod of Lewis.
Alexander MacLeod of Dunvegan.
Gilleganan MacNeill of Barray.
Ewin MacKinnon of Straguordell.

The MacQuarries followed the MacLeans. I have therefore placed them in the column in which MacLean Chiefs are mentioned. The MacIans were a branch of the MacDonalds.

This list enables us to form an idea of the territory included in the Lordship of the Isles. All the Western Islands belonged to the Lordship, and some territory on the mainland, namely, Garmoran, which included Moydart, Arisaig, Morar, and Knoydart, Ardgour, Ardnamurchan, Glenelg, Assynt, and Gairloch, which belonged to the MacLeods. Though Glengarry's country lies inland, he was a descendant of Somerled, and belonged to the great Clan Donald, so he acted with the Island Lord.

The formation of this powerful confederacy is the most important event in the history of the Western Clans, and distinguishes them from those on the mainland. The latter were joined together in such unions as that which formed the Clan Chattan, but none of these equalled in power the Lordship of the Isles, neither were they so firmly united as were the Western Clans.

Early in the fifteenth century the Lord of the Isles obtained a great accession of power. A little earlier, the O'Beolans, Earls of Ross, had become extinct in the male line. Mary Leslie, the grand-daughter of the last Earl, had become the heiress, and eventually her son Alexander, the Lord of the Isles, became Earl of Ross. The Regent was most unwilling to see this great earldom united to the Lordship of the Isles, realising that the possession of such vast power by one man would be a source of great danger to the kingdom at large. For this reason he resisted the claims of the Island Lord by all the means in his power, and the result was the Battle of Harlaw, which was fought in 1411. The Lord of the Isles after the battle became the de facto possessor of the Earldom, and in 1425 his claim was acknowledged by James I.

As time passed the Regent's fears were abundantly justified. These great feudatories of the Crown were filled with a new ambition ; they sought to make themselves absolutely independent, and to become monarchs themselves, owing obedience to no man. To attain this object, again and again they rose in rebellion against the King, and the consequence was that, during the whole of this troubled period, the Western clans were engaged in external warfare, just as they had been in earlier days.

In all these battles, at Bannockburn, Harlaw, Inverness, Inverlochy, and many other places, the Islanders were not opposed to rival clans armed, equipped & trained like themselves, but to armies, largely composed of cavalry, in which the knights, the men-at-arms, and the horses were protected by armour, which was well-nigh impenetrable by their missiles. As an old writer puts it, they had to attack a mobile wall of living steel.

We are told how they did it at Harlaw. They charged the wall of steel with splendid courage. Many were cut down, but the survivors fought their way into the very midst of the hostile army, ham-strung the horses with their dirks, grappled with the fallen riders as they struggled on the ground, sought out the joints in their harness, and through these they drove their daggers home, showing themselves to be a match even for the magnificent chivalry of Scotland. At Harlaw they lost 900 men, but, when night put a stop to the carnage, among them lay, dead and cold, 500 of Mar's mail-clad knights and men-at-arms.

Another important matter remains to be noted. When a mediæval Baron was constantly at war, his first thought was to maintain the fighting strength of his Barony at the highest possible level. Nothing would tend to diminish this more than dissentions among his vassals, and therefore he would exert himself to the utmost to prevent them from fighting with each other, or from entering into feuds with their neighbours.

It is probable that the four Barons did this in early days ; it is certain that the Lord of the Isles did so at a later period. He employed two methods : he mediated between any of the Chiefs who were quarrelling with each other, using all his authority to prevent a war from breaking out ; and when he did not himself require their services in his own wars, in order to keep the turbulent spirits over whom he ruled occupied, he organised a series of raids on the Orkneys. These began in 1418, and were the subjects of bitter complaints from the Earls of those islands.   The most important of them took place in 1460, when MacLeod of Dunvegan, " and the young gentlemen of the Isles " went on such an expedition.

Consequently I believe that, while the Island chiefs were under the control of feudal superiors who were really able to exercise full authority over them—that is, roughly speaking, between the years 1275 and 1475—though the clans were frequently engaged in external warfare, the Western Isles were enjoying peace and quiet.

I only know of two occasions on which the tranquility of the Islands was seriously disturbed during the fourteenth century.   About 1320 the MacLeods were at war with the Frasers, and between 1390 and 1400 the Lord of the Isles was consolidating his confederacy, and severe fighting took place between him and the Dunvegan Chief, who had refused to acknowledge him as his superior Lord.   In 1431 the Royal forces invaded Skye and occupied Sleat, but I am under the impression that during the first three-quarters of the fifteenth century there were no serious clan feuds.   There may have been some minor disturbances ; indeed, the records of a few have come down to us, but the authority exercised by the Lord of the Isles and his Council was powerful enough to prevent any serious outbreaks from taking place.   Scott, in his " Tales of a Grandfather," draws an appalling picture of the conditions of anarchy and misery in which most of the kingdom was then plunged, and, strange as it seems to us with our preconceived ideas as to unceasing warfare in the Highlands, I think that probably the Western Isles were in a more peaceful and prosperous state at this period than any other district in the realm.

But this state of affairs was not destined to last.   About 1475, the Island Lordship was rent in twain.   The intrigues in which John, Earl of Ross and Lord of the Isles, had been engaged with Edward of England a few years earlier, came to the knowledge of the Scottish Government.   The Earl was pronounced a traitor, and his estates were forfeited.   He submitted to the King, he was pardoned, and he was restored to the Island Lordship, but was forced to surrrender the Earldom of Ross.

At this submission his son and heir, Angus, was furious, and rose in rebellion against his father. Some of the clans supported the old Lord ; some, specially the different branches of the great Clan Donald, took sides with his son. After many less important battles between the rival clans, about 1480—the exact date is uncertain—a great naval battle was fought in a bay on the north coast of Mull, since known as the Bloody Bay, in which all the West Highland clans were engaged on one side or the other. In this battle the old Lord of the Isles was defeated and taken prisoner. Angus, the old Lord's victorious son, hastened to take vengeance on all those who had supported his father. He, however, was assassinated by an Irish harper some time before 1490. The old Lord of the Isles then recovered his estates, but gave over his authority to his nephew, Sir Alexander of Lochalsh, who rose in rebellion, and endeavoured to regain the Earldom of Ross. This led to the final forfeiture of the Island Lordship in 1493. The old Lord then retired into the Monastery of Paisley, where he died in 1498.

Legally the Lordship of the Isles at this time ceased to exist ; but it was the one all-absorbing desire of the Island Chiefs to see it restored in the person of Donald Dubh, the son of Angus Oig. He was at the time of the forfeiture a prisoner in the hands of the Government, but their loyalty to him was no less remarkable than that which their successors displayed towards the Royal House of Stuart, and during the fifty years which followed the forfeiture they rose in rebellion four times against the King, hoping that by doing so they would bring about the restoration of the Island Lordship. This, however, was the one thing the King was determined to prevent ; all the risings were suppressed, and after the Lords of the Isles became extinct in the direct line, no further efforts were made to restore the ancient Lordship.

Meanwhile a new and terrible era had begun in the history of the Isles. In the civil war between John, Lord of the Isles, and his son, great injuries and wrongs had been inflicted and endured ; the Chiefs were full of angry passions against each other ; there was no Lord of the Isles to mediate between them, and the dreadful period, during which the clan feuds were raging, began, and lasted during the next 120 years.

It would be impossible to make a complete list of these feuds, but the following record will give some idea of what the state of affairs in the Islands was. Concerning all of these feuds, except three, there is authentic documentary evidence. Those three depend on tradition, and I have marked them with an asterisk :—

* About 1480.—Clan Ranald attacked the MacLeods in Skye.

* About 1483.—The MacDonalds invaded and conquered Trotternish.

In 1501.—The MacLeans and the Camerons were at war.

1501-1506.—Donald Dubh's insurrection was going on.

1513-1519.—Sir Donald of Loch Alsh was in rebellion.

1528.—War broke out between the MacLeods of Dunvegan and the MacDonalds of Sleat.

1529.—The Macdonalds and MacLeans attacked the Campbells.

1539.—The MacDonalds of Sleat and the Mackenzies of Kintail were at mortal strife.

1539.—The MacDonalds of Islay and the MacLeans of Dowart commenced a long war.

1544.—The Frasers and Clan Ranald fought the Battle of Kinloch Lochy.

1545.—Donald Dubh's rebellion took place.

1561.—MacLean of Dowart was in arms against MacLean of Coll.

1561-1564.—For a long time the lands of Rinns, in Islay, had been in dispute between the MacLeans of Dowart and the MacDonalds of Islay. There had been fighting between them in 1539. This was now renewed.

1569.—Mackintosh and Keppoch were at war.

1581.—Glengarry and Kintail fell out.

*1581.—A frightful feud, which lasted a long time, was raging between the MacLeods of Dunvegan and Clan Ranald.

1585.—War between the Camerons and the Mackintoshes was raging.

1585.—The feud between the MacLeans and MacDonalds of Islay broke out afresh, and, as the MacLeods and the Camerons joined the former, and the MacDonalds of Sleat the latter, this was, perhaps, the most terrible feud of all.

1588.—The MacLeans attacked the MacIans.

1595.—About this time MacLeod of Dunvegan invaded Coigeach and Loch Broom, estates belonging to Kintail.

1598.—The MacAllasters and the MacDonalds were at variance.

1599.—The MacDonalds of Sleat and the MacLeods of Dunvegan were engaged for a long time in a war, which reduced both clans to the verge of ruin.

Besides these wars between rival clans, in individual communities there were several cases of disputed succession, which caused civil wars to take place. In one of these the Chief of the Camerons was murdered ; in another Ian Dubh, a monster of inquity, committed a succession of murders in order to make himself Chief at Dunvegan. But the worst of all occurred in Lewis, where anarchy reigned for something like 40 years, and unheard-of atrocities were committed.

These wars were prosecuted with relentless ferocity, and the slaughter on the field of battle was tremendous. It will suffice to describe three battles, the records of which have come down to us.

About 1530, Donald Gruamach of Sleat, and Allan of Moydart, the Clan Ranald Chief, invaded the MacLeod country in Skye. They landed at Loch Eynort, ravaged Minginish, Bracadale, and Duirinish up to the very gates of Dunvegan,

6

and swept on into Glendale. Alasdair Crottach, the Chief of the MacLeods, was in Harris when the invasion took place, but, as soon as he heard the news, he hastened to the scene of action, and called his clan together to meet the foe. He was joined by MacLeod of Lewis, so four of the most powerful clans in the Islands were engaged in this strife.

Macleod occupied an impregnable position facing the MacDonalds, and lay there for ten days till his last reinforcements had come up. Then he attacked the enemy. A tremendous struggle ensued, and things went badly for the MacLeods, hundreds of them were killed, and irretrievable disaster seemed imminent. The Chief's mother was present, and she ordered the fairy flag* to be displayed. The sight of the wizard banner of their clan gave the MacLeods fresh spirit; they renewed the combat with intense fury, and both sides suffered great losses. Allan of Moydart broke the MacLeod line, cutting off the Chief and the band of survivors who guarded the magic flag from the rest of the clan. But, at this moment, Donald Gruamach was killed by Murdo MacCaskill. The head of the MacDonald Chief was cut off, and raised on a spear, so that all men could see it. Immediately the MacLeod pipers played the MacDonald Lament. At the sound of this ill omened music, the MacDonalds were seized with a panic and began to give way on all sides. Allan of Moidart made desperate efforts to rally them, fighting himself with the utmost valour. He quickly avenged Donald's death, killing MacCaskill and his three brothers with his own sword; but all his efforts were vain, and he was compelled to retreat with the remnant of his followers. The MacLeods were so weakened by their losses that they could not pursue their enemies, and the MacDonalds eventually reached Loch Eynort, and embarked in their galleys.

Such was the slaughter in this battle, that the ravens, which stood on " Creagan nan Fitheach " (the Rock of the Ravens) drank the blood and ate the flesh of the slain, who were piled in heaps around, without descending from their

---

* According to tradition this flag had been given to MacLeod by the fairies in the fourteenth century with the promise that on three occasions, the waving of it would bring supernatural power to save the clan in times of great peril. It is still preserved at Dunvegan. Full details concerning the flag are given in the " MacLeods of Dunvegan." The battles of Glendale and Trompan are also described in this work.

airy perch. The seannachies say that this was the most
tremendous battle which was ever fought in the Western
Isles, and that both victors and vanquished were crippled for
years by the losses they had sustained.

In his history (page 161), Gregory describes a battle, which
was fought in 1544 at Loch Lochy, between Lord Lovat and
Clan Ranald :—" The contest began with the discharge of
arrows at a distance, but, when their shafts were spent, both
parties rushed to the combat, and attacking each other furi-
ously with their two-handed swords and battle axes, a dreadful
slaughter ensued." The Frasers were defeated, surrounded,
and cut to pieces. Out of three hundred men, only one gentleman, Fraser of Foyers, and four clansmen survived this
bloody day, and the Macdonalds lost almost as heavily.

About 1580, Clan Ranald, with a large force, landed at
Trompan, in Skye. He found the MacLeods in church. He
surrounded the sacred building, threw burning brands on the
thatched roof, and set it on fire. The whole congregation
lost their lives, some being burnt, some being cut down as
they rushed out. One woman escaped, and carried the news
to Dunvegan. The Chief gathered all the men he could, and
rushed forward to meet the enemy. A terrific battle took
place. One tradition says that the fairy flag was again waved.
The MacDonalds were driven back, and tried to launch their
galleys. One was launched, and her crew escaped, but the
tide was low, the galleys were high and dry in the bay, and it
was impossible to get them into the water. The MacDonalds
put up a desperate defence, but large reinforcements had
come up to join the MacLeods ; the former were greatly out-
numbered, and before the night came they were all killed.
Their bodies were laid in a long row beneath a dyke, and the
dyke overturned upon them. The battle is called " Blar
Milleadh Garaidh," The Battle of the Destruction of the
Dyke.

These descriptions may give us some idea of what clan
warfare was like. One would have thought that such battles
as these would have satisfied the souls of the most ardent
warriors, but it is on record that many of the islanders,
not content with all this fighting at home, went to Ireland

to take part in the wars which were constantly going on there. In 1545, a Highland army assisted Surrey, who commanded the troops of Henry VIII. in that country ; and in 1595, Hugh MacDonald of Sleat, and Rory MacLeod of Dunvegan each took 500 men to aid the Red O'Donnell and Shane O'Neil in their rebellion against Queen Elizabeth.

I gather that such expeditions to Ireland were not uncommon from a report on the state of the Islands, which was written about 1590, for the information of James VI. In this report the following rule is given :—" And in raising or furthbringing of thair men, ony time of zeir, to quhatsumever cuntrie or weiris (wars), na labourers of the ground are permittit to steir furth of the cuntrie, quhatever their maister have ado, except only gentlemen quhilkis labouris not, that the labour of teiling thair ground, and wynning thair corns may not be left undone, albeit thai byde furth ane haill zeir, as offtymes it happins quhen any of thair particular islands has to do with Irland or neighbours."

When we remember that one Lord of the Isles took 10,000 men with him to Harlaw in 1411 ; that another took 4000 men with him to Ireland in 1545, and that there were 1000 MacLeods at Worcerster, it becomes difficult to believe that this rule was habitually obeyed, and that only " gentlemen " were engaged on those distant expeditions.

While these frightful feuds were raging the Islands were in a terrible state, and the sufferings endured by the people were appalling.

In the raids which were constantly taking place, the homes of the people were burnt, their growing crops destroyed, their cattle and other live stock killed or carried off. Famine often stared them in the face, and they had to kill and eat their horses, dogs, and cats, to maintain life

Hand-fasting had to a great extent superseded marriage. Under this curious custom an agreement was made between two Chiefs that the son of one should live with the daughter of another as her husband for a year and a day ! If there were issue, or a prospect of issue, the union became permanent ; if there was no issue, each of the parties was at liberty to terminate the arrangement, and marry, or hand-fast, some one else. Though these irregular unions had not been blessed by the Church, the issue of them was held to be legitimate.

This not only aimed a blow at the sanctity of marriage, but was a fruitful cause of clan wars. When Donald Gorm MacDonald sent home his handfasted wife, who was a sister of MacLeod of Dunvegan, the latter declared that, though there had been no bonfires to celebrate the marriage, there should be some very fine ones to celebrate the divorce, and a feud was begun which brought both clans to the verge of ruin.

The Highlands had become a second cave of Adullam, to which resorted, as of old, " everyone that was in distress, and everyone that was in debt, and everyone that was discontented," and, it may be added, criminals of all descriptions, who had made their own countries too hot to hold them. The Chiefs were glad to welcome these turbulent spirits, as they added to the fighting strength of their clans, but, as they quartered them on their tenants, their presence was a heavy burden on the people of the country, and caused many difficulties.

Christianity had almost ceased to exist, most of the churches were burnt, and most of the clergy driven away.

As a consequence of all this the once kindly Highlanders had become possessed by an evil spirit of hatred and revenge, which showed itself in the dark deeds of revolting cruelty, deliberately planned and carried out in cold blood, concerning which so many dreadful stories are told. I do not love horrors, but to show how terrible the conditions were under which our forbears lived I relate three of these stories.

A party of twenty men who were crossing the Minch in a galley were forced to put into Loch Stockernish, on the east coast of Harris. Alasdair Dubh MacLeod, who lived there without asking who they were, received them with the greatest hospitality. At supper one of them let out that they were Clan Ranald MacDonalds. On hearing this their host slipped out, roused six of his men, and posted them well armed outside his door. He then came back and told his guests that, now he knew that they belonged to a hostile clan, he could no longer harbour them. The door was low and narrow, so that only one at a time could leave the house, and as each of these men passed out into the darkness he was struck down and killed by an unseen enemy.

Another tale relates how the MacGhittichs, a lawless tribe who lived in Harris, attacked the home of a man against whom they had a grudge. The man escaped, but, returning next day, found his wife and family all lying dead amid the smoking embers of his home. A fire still smouldered beneath a tripod which had been erected outside the house. Over this was hanging a pot ; in the pot were the remains of his infant grandson, who had been killed, cut in pieces, and boiled over the fire.

A party of MacLeods, who had been captured by the MacDonalds, were flung into a dungeon, and starved to death. It is said that they ate each other till not one was left. The story of the massacre of Eigg is so well-known that I need not do more than refer to it.

Criminals were punished with horrible severity. There are records of men being flogged to death, or flayed alive, of their homes being burnt, and their wives and children, down to the babe in arms, being utterly exterminated. A man who had planned the murder of Donald Gorm was dropped into a fearful dungeon at Duntulm, and left to die a hideous death from thirst.

I imagine that, during the sixteenth century, such a frightful state of anarchy prevailed in the country, that any trade there may have been at an earlier period was killed. The destruction wrought by the incessant raids of hostile clans must have been such that there was nothing to export, and, if there is nothing to export, nothing can be imported, for it is only by exports that imports can be paid for.

There was yet another cause at work which must have tended to check trade. Piracy on the high seas was now very common. About 1590, MacNeill of Barra went with a fleet of galleys to the coast of Ireland, where he did such dire mischief that complaints were made to Queen Elizabeth. She, in her turn, complained to the Scottish King. James employed Rory Mackenzie, afterwards tutor of Kintail, and he, by a trick, succeeded in capturing MacNeill. The chief was brought before the King, and, when charged with the piracies he had committed on Elizabeth's subjects, replied that he thought that he was doing the King a service by " annoying the woman who had killed his mother." His ready wit saved his life. In 1604, Rory MacLeod of Dunvegan had to pay £500 for " certaine wairs, guids and geir reft and spulzeit and tane from a bark in Loch Hourn in April 1587."

In 1625, Clan Ranald seized a Leith ship near Barra Head. As late as 1636 the same Chief plundered an English vessel, called the Susannah.

But were the Islands of the West really in such a dreadful state ? There are four descriptions of them written in the 16th century, one by Macgregor, Dean of Lismore ; one by Monro, also Dean of Lismore ; and two by anonymous authors. One of these mentions the massacre at Eigg, but with this exception, they say nothing about the condition in which the country was, and, indeed, they give so favourable an impression of the state of affairs there that one author, after reading them, expresses the opinion that the 16th century was the " golden age in West Highland History." But all four were writing a description of the Western Isles, not a history, and they probably thought that the condition of the country was beside the questions they wished to discuss.

One can imagine that a modern traveller, visiting some islands in the Pacific, though he knew they had been the scene of terrific battles between native tribes, might entirely pass over these, and only relate his own experiences. I do not think, therefore, that the silence of these writers as to the terrible conditions which I have described is any proof that they did not exist, and, indeed, the evidence is so overwhelming, that I do not consider that there can be any doubt on the subject.

The pacification of the West Highlands will be described in the next chapter. In order to complete the story of clan warfare, it is necessary to briefly refer to the campaigns, beginning in 1644, in which the clansmen fought with such splendid courage and devotion in the cause of the Royal House of Stuart. They were now again engaged in external warfare.

The history of these most gallant attempts to restore their rightful Kings to the throne has been written again and again, and it need not be repeated here, but the following very short sketch will bring home to the minds of my readers the whole-hearted devotion of the Western clans to the Royalist cause. Leaving out of account one or two less important efforts, such as the one which ended so disastrously at Loch Garry in 1654, and the still more unfortunate attempt in 1719, the clans were engaged in five really serious attempts on behalf of the Stuarts.

In 1644, the brilliant campaigns under Montrose made the great Marquess Master of Scotland, and filled him with hopes that he would be able to march into England, and establish his Royal master again on the throne, hopes which were dashed to the ground by the crushing defeat at Philip-haugh.

In 1651, a Highland army was with Charles II. in the South of Scotland, shared in the defeat at Dunbar, marched with the King into England, and was almost destroyed at Worcester, losing 13,000 men.

In 1689, many of the Chiefs responded to the appeals of James II., then in Ireland, and, under the command of Dundee, began the campaign so splendidly by winning the Battle of Killiecrankie. But, having lost their brilliant leader in that battle, their subsequent efforts under less capable commanders accomplished little or nothing.

In 1715 the Royal Standard was again raised at Braemar, and an army of Highlanders was gathered together, which, under Montrose or Dundee, might have done great things, but which, under Mar, accomplished nothing.

In 1745, the last, and perhaps the greatest, effort of all, was made. The Prince occupied Edinburgh, he marched into England as far as Derby. Some writers maintain that, had he pushed on to London, the Crown would have been won ; and yet it all ended in disaster at Culloden.

The Camerons and MacDonalds of Clanranald were engaged in all of these glorious, if unfortunate, enterprises. The Macleans took part in the first four, and were only pre-vented from joining Prince Charles in 1745 by the arrest of their Chief at Edinburgh in June 1745, charged with being in the service of the French King.

The Mackinnons joined in all, excepting the campaign which ended at Worcester.

The Mackenzies had their share in the battles fought by Montrose, they joined Lord Mar in 1715, and again rose in 1719.

The Macdonalds of Sleat were with Montrose, were present at Worcester, and fought under Lord Mar.

The MacLeods lost so heavily at Worcester that it was agreed among the other clans that they should not be asked to take part in any further enterprises till they had had time to recover. For various reasons they never again drew the sword in the cause of the Stuarts.

The loyalty of the Highlanders to the Stuarts is one of the most amazing paradoxes in history. For more than two centuries they had been constantly in a state of rebellion against Kings who belonged to the house of Stuart. In 1545 they had actually renounced their allegiance to one of these monarchs, and very reluctantly they had submitted to the Royal authority early in the seventeenth century. Then suddenly they turned round, they became intensely loyal, and were ready to sacrifice anything and everything in the King's service.

And it was not only the Chiefs who were full of loyalty to their King. Even among the clans which did not join the Prince in 1745, the feeling was intensely strong. Sir A. Mac-Donald, writing on September 5, 1745, says :—" I need not tell you the difficulty of recruiting 100 men. The men here are almost as fond of the young gentleman as their wives and daughters are." The young gentleman was the Prince, and Sir Alexander was trying to raise men to fight against him.

I am not sure that the paradox is as remarkable as it seems at first sight. The spirit of loyalty to a superior was deeply rooted in the character of the Islanders. In the 14th century, King Robert Bruce and his successors had no more faithful subjects than they. In the following century they transferred their allegiance to their own immediate superior, the

Lord of the Isles, and they remained faithful to him and his successors, not merely till the Lordship was forfeited, but until there was no scion of the house of Somerled in the direct line who claimed the dignity.

Though some of the Chiefs were firmly attached to Mary Queen of Scots, for a time the flame of loyalty burnt low in their hearts. But, when they saw their King fighting for his Crown against enemies, whose religious and political opinions they detested, when they saw him laying down his life on the scaffold, when they saw his son robbed of his inheritance, and driven into exile, all the generosity and romance in their natures caused the flame of devotion to the King to kindle anew in their hearts.

We need not be surprised that, when they beheld another King driven from his throne to find refuge at St Germains, their devotion to him, to his son, and to his grandson, became with them the passion of their lives, and that, again and yet again, they strove to place their Royal Master on the throne.

Why was it that none of these enterprises succeeded ? Probably ultimate success was not possible in any of them. The forces which were arrayed against the Stuarts on all these occasions were so strong that a few thousand Highlanders, however brave they might be, could not hope to overcome them. But there were contributory causes in the character of a Highland army. Their valour was indisputable, but the pride of the Chiefs, and the jealousy of each other which prevailed among them, made it very difficult for a general in command to exercise due control over them. Tradition says that at Harlaw the MacLeods refused to fight unless they were given the post of honour on the right wing, and, more than 300 years later, something of the same sort occurred, when the MacDonalds were put on the left wing of the Prince's army at Culloden. This is only one instance of the difficulties which were constantly arising. The officer in command of a Highland army required, not only military capacity, but infinite tact and judgment. Montrose and Dundee possessed these gifts. Buchan, Cannon, Middleton, Mar, even Lord George Murray, did not possess them, and, for lack of them, their leadership failed.

Another source of weakness in a Highland army was the desire of the men, when a battle had been won, to go home for a time, to see their families, to secure their crops, to dispose of any spoil they might have taken. Even Montrose could not prevent them from doing this. It was because so many men had left the army that he was defeated at Philiphaugh. Even if this habit did not lead to a defeat, it often made it impossible to secure the fruits of a victory, and was a source of weakness, which it is difficult to overestimate.

The failure of these efforts, certainly the failure in the '45, has given us a more splendid page of history than their success could have done. Had he been victorious the Prince might have been a stately figure as, robed in silk and satin, he stood in the Court of his triumphant father at St James's. But he showed himself a veritable hero as, clad in a ragged kilt, he sat in the boat of Donald MacLeod, of Gualtregill, his devoted pilot, bearing incredible hardships with unfailing courage, and cheering the spirits of his men with songs and jests, or again a little later as, clad this time in the dress of a Highland maid-servant, with Flora Macdonald as his companion, he crossed the Minch, and, by her help and guidance, eluded his foes.

But if the Prince was a splendid figure, all those who helped him were splendid figures, too. Not only Flora Mac-Donald, Donald MacLeod, and a host of others, without whose aid he must have been captured ; but all those who knew where he was, and who could have earned the £30,000 which the Government had offered for his capture. That no single Highlander tried to earn this shameful money is a source of pride to us all.

The fighting days of the Highlanders by no means came to an end at Culloden. In every war which has been waged since 1760, they have rendered splendid service to King and country. But they have been fighting as soldiers in the regular army, and the 16th of April 1746 was the last day on which they went into battle as clans, under the command of their Chiefs, wearing their distinctive tartans, and practising their old methods of warfare.

In 1745, the officers of the independent companies raised by MacLeod of Dunvegan were all of them his own clansmen. In 1780 the officers in the battalion raised and commanded by his grandson, were all of them professional soldiers transferred from other battalions to train the Highlanders according to the rules of the drill-book. This well illustrates the change which had taken place

CHAPTER VI

SCOTTISH KINGS AND ISLAND CHIEFS.

INTRIGUES OF THE ISLAND LORDS WITH ENGLAND—
POLICY OF THE KINGS—EFFORTS OF JAMES VI. TO
PACIFY THE ISLANDS—THE STATUTES OF IONA,
THEIR EFFECTS—BISHOP KNOX OF THE ISLES.

The Scottish Kings had grave and difficult problems to
solve in the West Highlands during the fifteenth century.
At that time the Island Lords were dreaming of making themselves quite independent, and hoped, as Macaulay says,
" to change their caps of maintenance for Royal Crowns."
To gain this end they and the Chiefs who followed them were
at intervals rising in rebellion against the King, entering into
conspiracies with discontented nobles in the South, and,
what was a greater source of danger than all, intriguing
with Scotland's arch enemies, the Sovereigns of England.

It is not necessary to describe all the rebellions which
took place, but it may bring the magnitude of the danger
home to the reader's mind if I relate the story of one intrigue
with England.

In October 1461, John, Earl of Ross and Lord of the
Isles, by the advice of his council sitting at Ardtornish Castle,
issued a commission to certain plenipotentiaries to confer
with the deputies of the English King. These ambassadors
went to London, and concluded a treaty which, though it
was signed at Westminster on February 13th, 1462, is known
as the " Treaty of Ardtornish." Under this treaty Scotland
was to be conquered by the Earls of Ross and Douglas with
the assistance of English troops, it was to be divided between
them, and each of them was to become the sworn vassal of
the English King. The events which followed, and the final
forfeiture of the Island Lordship in 1493, have been related
in Chapter V.

After the forfeiture had taken place the dangers which menaced the safety of the realm were no less acute. The Western Chiefs were longing to see the ancient Lordship of the Isles restored. Though they were engaged in desperate feuds amongst themselves, whenever they saw a favourable opportunity of attaining their great object, they forgot their quarrels, and uniting their forces, rose in rebellion against the King. In 1501, in 1514, and in 1528 such risings took place. These were suppressed with greater or less difficulty. In 1545, Donald Dubh, the heir of the Isles, who, after spending 40 years in captivity, had been set at liberty by the Earl of Arran, headed a yet more serious rebellion, and again entered into negotiations with the King of England.

On June 28, 1545, acting with the advice of the seventeen Chiefs who formed his council, he appointed plenipotentiaries to treat with Lennox, the representative of Henry VIII., and finally, a treaty having been made, he and all his vassals solemnly on August 5 took the oath of allegiance to the English Monarch.

The dangers with which the Scottish Sovereigns were face to face being so great, they not unnaturally thought that it was better to see the clans divided and fighting with each other than to see them united, and threatening the rest of the kingdom, and some of the measures which they adopted indicate that their real object was, not to allay strife, but to foment it.

They granted the same lands and offices to different Chiefs. In 1498, in charters granted by James IV. to the MacLeods of Dunvegan and to the MacLeods of Lewis, the same office, the Bailiary of Trotternish, was granted to both Chiefs. In a charter dated November 30th, 1542, James V. granted Sleat, Trotternish, and North Uist, which were in the possession of the MacDonalds, to Alexander MacLeod of Dunvegan. There are probably many other instances of the same thing being done in the histories of other clans. They also issued letters of fire and sword, in which they positively ordered one Chief to attack another. A specimen of one of these letters will be found a little further on.

It is difficult to find any other motive for such measures as these than a desire to set the Western Chiefs quarrelling amongst themselves.

Both Kings paid several visits to the Western Isles at the head of forces strong enough to enforce obedience for a time, and both of them were personally popular among the Chiefs, but so long as an heir in the direct line of the ancient house of the Isles remained in existence, nothing could undermine their devotion to him, and these monarchs did not succeed in arousing in the Chiefs any feeling of loyalty to themselves.

During the Regency which followed on the death of James V., during the troubled reign of Mary, and during the Regency which followed her dethronement, the Government in Scotland could spare but little attention for so remote a corner of the kingdom, and things were allowed to take their course in the Isles of the West.

When, in 1583, James VI. took the reins of government into his own hands, some material changes had taken place in the situation. The West Highlands were still in a state of frightful anarchy, but the point of view from which the Government regarded this was altered.

Fifty years earlier that anarchy had been considered to be the least of two evils. Now, the greater of these two had disappeared. There was no longer any reason to fear that the once powerful Lordship of the Isles could be restored under one head, and again become a menace to the safety of the realm. Donald Gorm of Sleat claimed descent from the ancient Lords, but in the direct line the house of the Isles was extinct, and in any case, now that the clans had been at war with each other for more than a century, such bitter feelings had been engendered among them, that it would have been impossible to unite them in any common enterprise. The greater evil having passed away, men began to realise how terrible the lesser one had now become. They saw that it was causing great material loss to the nation, that little or no revenue was being derived from the Islands, and that in case of war it was not likely that the Royal army would be strengthened by any contingents from the Western Isles.

But this was not all.   The state of affairs in that part
of the country was a source of disgrace and shame to its ruler.
The business of a Government is to govern, and, if it cannot
do so, it does not justify its existence.   James certainly
could not govern the Western clans ; they were making war
on each other without let or hindrance from him, they were
committing atrocities which shocked all who heard of them,
his writ did not run in the islands, and his authority was
daily being set at nought and defied.

There is no reason to doubt that James was extremely
anxious to pacify the Islands, but his main reason for wishing
to do so was that he hoped in this way to replenish his depleted
treasury by obtaining large contributions to the revenue from
his West Highland vassals.

But how could he accomplish his end ?   He had neither
the money, the military force, nor the strength of character,
which would have enabled him to conquer the country.
It cannot be said of him that he allowed matters to drift,
and he was obliged to use less drastic means, but during the
next thirty years he was constantly doing something to
attain his object.

In 1585 he put in operation a plan which his grandfather
had occasionally pursued and found useful.   He insisted
that each Chief should send some of his nearest kinsmen
to live in the South, as hostages for the peaceable behaviour
of his clan.   The presence of these hostages was not only
a guarantee for the good conduct of their Chief, but it was
also a means of civilising and educating the hostages themselves.   Judged by our standards, the Scottish Capital
was itself in a turbulent and disorderly condition, but its
civilisation was far more advanced than that of the Western
Highlands.   A sojourn in Edinburgh must have had a great
effect in opening the minds of those who were forced to
live there, and it undoubtedly gave them a knowledge of the
Southern tongue.

In 1587 was passed an Act, known as the " General
Band."   Under this every Chief was made responsible
for injuries done by his dependants.   In the Muniment
Room at Dunvegan is an interesting paper, which illus-

trates the effect of this provision. In a year, which is not named, a number of men from Glenelg " did wrang, in their wrangous, violent, and masterful spoliation and away taking fra the complenar, furth of his merchant buith in Inverness, of the particular quantities of guids, geir, and merchandise, particularlie under wrethin, of the guids under-specefiit." Then follows a list of the goods stolen, with prices attached, too long to quote, and for the large sums involved the Chief was held to be liable.

In 1588 James found himself in a serious difficulty. The war about the Rinns of Islay between the MacDonalds and the MacLeans, which had been going on for so long, broke out again. MacLean was in favour with the King, and the latter wanted to help him, but he had no forces at his disposal, and he took an absolutely fatal step, which, had he reflected for a single moment, he must have seen would indefinitely delay the attainment of his main object, the pacification of the Islands. He issued a letter of fire and sword to MacLeod of Dunvegan, ordering him to support MacLean. His motive was probably not the one which had actuated his predecessors when they did the same thing, but the results of his action were no less disastrous. James may have issued several such letters. The one to MacLeod is in the Muniment Room at Dunvegan, and I give a copy of it :—

" Traist friend we greit you weill. Understanding that some invasion and violent persute has laitlie been usit be the Clan Donald upoun our weill belovit Lauchlane McClayne of Dowart, his freindis and servandis, and yat they intend to attempt furder injure agains him, and, so far as in thame yis, to wrak him, his haill friendis and servandis, landis and possessionis, he being or trew faithful and obedient subject, readie, at all occasionis, to hazard his lyfe, landis and heritage in the maintenance and furth setting of our authoritie and service, we are movit thair fore maist affec-tunslie to requeist and desire you that ye concur, and give your assistance to the said Lauchlane in resisting of the violence and persute of the said Clan Donald, and supplie him with you haill freindis and forse agains quhatsumevir

7

uther personis, his enemies and unfreindis, sall meine indirectly to cause him trouble, or to invaid him by way of deid. As ye will do us maist acceptable plesour and service and report our special thankis, and we commit you to God from Striuiling Castle the xxix. day of September 1588.

" JAMES R."

In the following year James was guilty of a most disgraceful breach of good faith, which made it impossible for anyone henceforth to trust him. He induced the Chiefs of Dowart, Dunyveg, and Sleat to come to Edinburgh under a safe conduct, that he might discuss with them the terms on which this war might be brought to an end. The moment they were in his power, he seized their persons, and kept them prisoners in Edinburgh Castle until they had each of them paid heavy fines. During the next nine years one or two ill-planned and futile expeditions were sent to the Islands, but these accomplished nothing.

In 1597 the Chiefs were ordered to produce the title-deeds of their estates before May 1598 on pain of forfeiture. This was a singularly ill-advised measure. Many of the title-deeds had been lost during the long period of internal trouble through which the Highlands had passed, and some loyal and well-disposed Chiefs were goaded into rebellion by the order to produce documents which could not be found. Among the estates forfeited under the Act of 1597 were those belonging to the MacLeods of Lewis. James seized the opportunity to try his favourite plan for the pacification of the Island. He granted Lewis to some Lowland gentlemen, who were known as the Fife Adventurers, and when they failed, to another group of Lowlanders. The coming of these gentlemen to Lewis only made the confusion there worse confounded, and after ten years of strenuous effort the last of them gave up the enterprise as hopeless.

In 1608 James sent an expedition under Lord Ochiltree to the Highlands, and, unlike his previous efforts, this did have some effect. The Castles of Dunyveg and Dowart were taken. The following Western Chiefs came to meet Lord Ochiltree at Aros :—MacDonald of Dunyveg, MacLean of Dowart, his brother Lauchlane, Donald Gorm of Sleat, Clan

Ranald, Rory MacLeod of Dunvegan, and some other gentle-men. All these, Lord Ochiltree reported, placed themselves at his disposal unconditionally. It appears, however, from a contemporary author, that they were not so complaisant as Lord Ochiltree tried to make out.

Finding fair words of no avail, Ochiltree asked the Chiefs to come on board his ship, the Moon, to hear a sermon from the Bishop of the Isles, and to dine afterwards. All accepted the invitation except Rory MacLeod, who suspected some sinister design. The result showed his wisdom. Ochiltree, when dinner was done, announced to his guests that they were his prisoners, and sailed with them to Ayr, whence he took them to Edinburgh, and presented them to the Council. This was another shameful breach of good faith.

The fact that so many of the Chiefs were in the King's hands greatly facilitated the execution of a new plan which was formed in 1609. The Bishop of the Isles was sent as Commissioner to the Highlands. The imprisoned Chiefs were liberated on finding security that they would concur with the bishop in his proposed plans, and the latter was empowered to grant the Chiefs still at liberty a safe conduct if they met him at Iona.

About the end of July 1609, twelve of the most powerful Chiefs met the bishop at Iona in solemn conclave. and, with the consent of the assembled Chiefs, the nine Statutes of Iona were drawn up, which provided for the future government of the Highlands.

Omitting less important details, the following provisions were made in these famous statutes :—

Clan wars were to cease, and all future disputes were to be settled by the laws of the realm.

Churches were to be built, the number of the clergy increased, due respect shewn to them, and their stipends regularly paid.

The Chiefs, and all their tenants, who owned more than sixty cows, were to send their children to be educated in the South.

Handfasting was declared to be illegal. (See Chapter V.).

Sorning was to be put down, and criminals among the sorners were to be tried and punished. (See Chapter III.).

The sale of wine and brandy was made illegal.

It was made a crime to carry fire-arms.

What seems a hard statute was directed against the bards. I suppose that it was thought that they incited the clans to war.

The Chiefs, as before, were to send hostages for their good conduct South, and to appear before the Council themselves on July 16 in each year. Disobedience would be followed by forfeiture.

For the observance of the Statutes, the Bishop took a strict bond from all the Chiefs present, and some of them entered into bonds of friendship with each other. One of these, between Donald Gorm MacDonald of Sleat and Rory MacLeod of Dunvegan, is preserved in the Dunvegan charter chest. It is dated at Icolmekill in August 1609. I give some extracts.—

" Forsameikle as the foresaidis personis, being certanelie persuadit of their dreid Soverane His Majestie's clemencie and mersye towardis thame, and willing of thair reform-atioun and thair leiving hereafter in peace, as his Hienes quyet, modest, and pecable subjectis. And the saidis parties, considering the godles and unhappie turnis done by ayer of yame, yair freindis, servandis, tenants, dependaris and partakeris to utheris, quhilkis from yair hairtis yai and ilk ane of yame now repentis. Thairfoir the saidis parteis fra yair heairts ffreilie remittis dischargis, and forgivis, ilk ane of yame, utheris, and thair foresaidis, for all and quhat-sumevir slauchteris murthoris, heirshippis, spuilseis of guidis, and raising of fyre, committit be ayer of thame agains utheris, yair freyndis, tenantis, and dependaris, at onie time preceiding the dait heirof. And furder the saidis pairteis faythfullie promittis bindis and obleiss thame to leif heir-efter (be the grace of God) in Christiane societie and peace, and ilk ane to assist and maintain utheris in yair honest and leesum effairies and busynes."

It could not be expected that a single stroke of the pen could at once change customs which had been practised for centuries, and there were some troubles in the Highlands during the next few years. A dispute as to the succession to the Chiefship of the MacNeils disturbed Barra. A claim by Argyle to the superiority of Lochiel's Lochaber estate disturbed that district. In 1614 the MacDonalds of Islay rose in rebellion, in 1625 there was serious trouble with the MacIans of Ardnamurchan; but this was the last case of internal warfare in the Western Isles. Most of the Chiefs who had agreed to the Statutes of Iona remained true to their engagements, and duly presented themselves before the Council each year.

In 1616 they entered into a fresh agreement. In this the Statutes of Iona were renewed, and some fresh ones added. These last may be summarised as follows :—The number of gentlemen each Chief might henceforth maintain in his household was limited, in MacLean's case to eight, in Clan Ranald's and MacLeod's to six, in others to three. Their dwelling-places were fixed, and they were to make " policie and planting " about their houses. They were to let their lands at fixed rents, instead of the exactions which had before been demanded. (See Chapter III.).

With the signing of the Statutes of Iona a new era of peace and obedience to law opened in the Highlands. Henceforth the disputes of the Chiefs were settled, not by the sword, but by the laws of the realm. I give three instances of this.

For at least two hundred years, a dispute between the MacDonalds and MacLeods as to the ownership of North Uist, Sleat, and Trotternish, had been raging, and oceans of blood had been shed in ever recurring attempts to settle it by force of arms. In 1617 this dispute was submitted to the courts of law, and their decision was loyally accepted by both Chiefs.

In 1622 the MacDonalds of Clan Ranald, instigated by the wife of Donald Gorm, attacked St Kilda, seized and carried away all the cattle and other property of the Islanders, burnt their houses, and spared only their lives.

One can imagine what would have happened a few years earlier. The fiery cross would have been sent round, the clan collected, the galleys manned, the enemy's country invaded, and a devastating war commenced which might have lasted for years, and cost hundreds of lives.

Now, as appears in a letter from Sir Rory MacLeod to Lord Binning, which is among the public records, the Chief appealed to the Government for redress, and not one drop of blood was shed.

In 1630 a " cryminal information " was laid before the Justice, at the instance of John MacLeod of Dunvegan, the object of which was to secure the punishment of some criminals by process of law.

A number of men, whose names are given, came in the month of May from Lord Lovat's estate in Glenelg to Arnistel " and yr killit thrie ky wyth calfys, belonging to Jon McConal, windit (wounded), and struck dyvers uther goods to the death. Secondlie the foirnamit personis cam in the moneth of June to the foirsaid toun, and maliciously brack ye said Jon McConal his house yr, and thifteously tuik away wyth thame threttie stanes butter and cheis, wyth the coltir, and uther his plenth and graith (furniture) with dyvers plenishing. Thirdlye they maliciously brack Christine Nene Finlay hir house and barn, and tuik away threttie or fourtie stanes butter and cheis, wyth sum wedders, 20 merks in money, ane boll meall, ane kist, and twa great criels yat keepit the meat, with a twa arit (oared) boat. Fourthlie they tuik and apprehendit Christine Neyn and Jon Vic Kenneth in Glenelg, uponn the kingis his way, yea in the mean tyme going to thir leisum (lawful) effairis, and yr put violent handis on the said Christine, cruellis tirrit (stripped) hir mother nakeit, wyth hir children, and tuik away with thame all yair closis, wyth ane kaittill, and twelff elnes lining, thereafter doing and brusseing her to the perrell of her lyfe. Through committing of whilk crimes, the haill landis ar laid waist, and the country disturbit, so that no man cannot saiflie pas to do his leisom effairis."

These instances of appeals being made to the law all occur in the history of one clan. I do not doubt that similar cases occur in the records of other clans, and that the acceptance by the chiefs of the Statutes of Iona brought about equally beneficial results throughout the whole of the West Highlands.

The reign of law had begun, and in a marvellously short space of time, the most remarkable results were seen.

As the herds of cattle increased, a prosperous trade sprang up, and great droves of cattle went South every year for sale in the Southern markets. The first man to take a drove to Falkirk was one of the most redoubtable warriors of the Clan Donald, Donald MacIan Mhic Shamuis, who had greatly distinguished himself in war early in the century, and now showed himself to be no less vigorous in his new avocation.

During the next few years the value of the land in the West Highlands was multiplied by more than forty times, and the West Highlands enjoyed a prosperity and well-being to which they had been strangers for centuries.

Gradually the Highlanders, who had been on the verge of absolute paganism in the 16th century, became, possibly, the most religious and God-fearing people in the world.

In the 18th century the ignorant Islesmen, who could not previously have read their " neck verse " to save their lives, possessed a system of education which put to shame that which was found in highly civilised England.

As time went on, the clansmen, whose valour had been wasted in hundreds of ferocious clan battles, became the mainstay of their King and country, and the Highland regiments won never-dying glory on innumerable stricken fields of battle.

Since the Mother country began to send her children to people her daughter lands, no emigrants have done more to create and maintain a great and loyal colonial Empire than the Highlanders, and all over the world they have won the respect and admiration of their neighbours. I firmly believe that we owe these great blessings to the work which was done when the Statutes of Iona were signed in 1609.

We may well ask ourselves why this effort to pacify the Highlands succeeded when all previous ones had failed ? I believe that the main credit is due to Bishop Knox of the

Isles. He was a man of rare tact and judgment, and he was gifted with very remarkable powers of persuasion. He reasoned with the chiefs, he pointed out to them the appalling condition of distress and misery to which the incessant wars of the last hundred years had reduced their country, and he found that they were not inaccessible to reason.

It must be remembered that they were not the totally uneducated men their fathers had been. Their signatures attached to the bonds of friendship show that they could write. They were not incapable of understanding the force of the arguments which were put before them, and, though they probably surrendered with reluctance their independence, and their right to make peace and war, they did surrender them, and the Statutes of Iona, the Magna Charta of the Highlands, were agreed to.

The names of the men who accomplished this work should live in our grateful recollection, specially the name of Andrew Knox, Bishop of the Isles. It is probable that he conferred greater and more lasting benefits on the West Highlanders than any other man who has ever been concerned in the management of their affairs.

CHAPTER VII.

THE PASSING OF THE OLD ORDER.

THE REFORMATION—EPISCPOACY IN THE ISLANDS—EDU-
CATION, TRADE, ESTATE MANAGEMENT—CROFTERS—
THE CLAN SYSTEM IN FORCE UP TO 1745—DESTROYED
IN 1747—LOVE OF PEOPLE FOR CHIEFS—PATRIARCHAL
SYSTEM DESTROYED ABOUT 1770—THE RESULTS.

While the events described in the last two chapters
were taking place throughout the West Highlands, the
Reformation was proceeding in the South of Scotland. The
Roman Catholic Church was practically overthrown in the
days of Queen Mary and John Knox, but a struggle almost
immediately commenced in the Reformed Church between the
Episcopalians and the Presbyterians.

We are so accustomed to think of Scotland as a purely
Presbyterian country, that we forget the strength of Episcopacy in the seventeenth century. At least half the population were Episcopalians, possibly more than half, and the
influence they possessed is indicated by the fact that for
something like sixty years in that century, the Episcopalian
form of religion was the Established Church of Scotland.

But the Presbyterians were also strong, and at times
they completely overcame their rivals. In 1592, Presbyterianism was established as the National Religion of Scotland.
In 1606 the Bishops were restored, and in 1610 Episcopacy
entirely triumphed ; in 1638 it again fell, but was once more
restored about 1662, only to fall again finally after the Revolution. It is probable that the Reformation did not come to
the Islands till after Episcopacy had become the form of
religion established in the country. Some of the Chiefs
clung to the old religion, notably Clan Ranald, but most of
them became Episcopalians.

It is clear that at this period Episcopalian clergy were
ministering to the spiritual needs of the people. Among the

papers at Dunvegan is an appointment by the Bishop dated
in 1631 to the parish of Oynert in Skye, and some tacks of
tiends beginning in 1623 from the Bishops of Argyle and the
Isles.

There is very ample evidence that the West Highlanders
were sincerely attached to their Episcopal Mother Church.
This became very obvious when Episcopacy was abolished
and Presbyterianism set up as the national form of religion
after the Revolution of 1688. During the following years
many Episcopalian clergymen were forcibly ejected, and
Presbyterians installed in their places. These proceedings
aroused the bitterest resentment, and it was only slowly
and by degrees that the West Highlanders became reconciled
to the Presbyterian form of worship. It is a curious fact
that they have now completely forgotten that they were
once Episcopalians.

It is possible that the attachment of the West Highlanders to the Episcopal Church may have had something to
do with their devotion to the Stuart Kings. When James
VI. was asked to give his reason for supporting the Episcopal
Church, he gave it in one short pithy sentence—" No Bishop,
no King." There was clearly the idea in his mind that the
Monarchical and Episcopalian systems were based on similar
principles, and he may not have been entirely mistaken. At
all events, it is certainly the case that the enemies of Charles
I. and of his successors were generally Independents or Presbyterians, while the Royalists and Jacobites were either Roman
Catholic or Episcopalian.

There is ample evidence that the clergy met with considerable success in raising the people from the semi-heathen
state into which they had fallen in the previous century.
The West Highlanders are naturally a religious people, and
when the dreadful spirit of hatred and revenge, which had
been engendered by the clan feuds, passed away, religion
gradually reassumed its power. Martin Martin describes
them as saying grace after meals, and adding to their grace a
petition for their Chief's welfare. None but a genuinely
religious people would do this.

Turning from ecclesiastical matters to secular, we find
that in the first half of the 17th century, as time went on,
fresh developments were taking place in many directions.
One of the Statutes of Iona had ordered that the Chiefs,
and every man who owned 60 cows, should send their children
to be educated in the South.   Among the bills at Dunvegan
are several for the " buird and entertainment " of the Chief's
sons at Glasgow, where they were being educated at the
University.   The earliest of these is dated in 1622.   Possibly
a little later, the Chieftains began to send their sons to schools
in the South, and, by the middle of the century, the gentlemen
of the Isles were a well-educated class.   Possibly this accounts
for their having become the well-bred, courteous set of men
that they certainly were during the latter half of the seventeenth century.

I repeat here a quotation in which Macaulay gives a
description of them :—" It must in fairness be acknowledged
that the patrician virtues were not less widely diffused among
the Highlanders than the patrician vices.   There was no
other part of the Kingdom where such men had in such a
degree the better qualities of an aristocracy, grace and dignity
of manner, self-respect, and that noble sensibility which
makes dishonour more terrible than death.   A gentleman
of Skye or Lochaber would do the honours of his home with
a lofty courtesy worthy of the splendid circle of Versailles."

The education of the humbler classes came later, but it
began much earlier in Scotland than it did in England.   In
1696 and 1708, Education Acts were passed ; in 1701 the newly-
founded S.P.C.K. took up the work of education.   From
early in the century I find in the estate accounts payments
to schoolmasters.   The estate contributed about £5 a year
towards the salary of each teacher, and every tacksman was
bound under the conditions of his lease to make a certain
payment for the same purpose.   S.P.C.K. paid salaries to
teachers of £10 to £20 a year.   Other teachers only received
from £6 to £11 2s 2d

I imagine that girls shared in these educational advantages, but Martin, whom I have so often quoted, says " that
women were anciently denied the use of writing in the Islands

to prevent love intrigues ; their parents believed that nature
was too skilful in that matter, and needed not the help of
education, and therefore writing would be of dangerous
consequences to the weaker sex."

Both Parliament and S.P.C.K., up to 1767, insisted that
English should be the language in which the teaching was to
be given. It is difficult to understand how efficient instruction could be given in a language of which the children were
entirely ignorant.

Gaelic was undoubtedly the language of the people. In
the report on Harris, dated 1772, to which I have so often
referred, it is expressly stated that out of the 1993 inhabitants, only one hundred could speak English.

No doubt the Chiefs and tacksmen spoke both languages.
Most of the Chiefs, however, lost their Gaelic in the eighteenth
century, as they were educated in the South, but some of them
appear to have been anxious that their children should learn
Gaelic. Sir A. Macdonald says, in a letter written in 1744,
that his "son Jamie is getting more Gallick at Kingsburgh
than tongue can tell."

It is worthy of note that from the census return of 1921
it appears that 48 per cent. of the people of the County of
Inverness still speak both Gaelic and English, and that 4443
persons speak no other tongue than Gaelic.

Trade with the outside world was beginning to flourish.
The most important exports were the great droves of cattle
which were annually sent South from every estate in the
country. The cattle from the Outer Isles must certainly
have performed part of the journey by sea, but those from
Skye were taken to Kyleakin or Kyle Rhea, ferried across
the Sound, and went by land to Falkirk. This implies that
fairly peaceable conditions prevailed at this period on the
mainland. An old account book shows that the cost of send-
ing a drove of cattle South in 1670 was £13 18s 0d. This
included the expenses of eleven men and horses from Skye
to Falkirk and back, a sum of £7 for " customs and otherwise "
—probably the auctioneer's charges for selling the cattle,
and the wages of the men employed.

It is likely that other commodities, such as cloth, blanketing, butter and cheese, began to be exported at the same time. On the other hand, the bills in the Muniment Room at Dunvegan, which begin about 1600, show that clothes and many other articles were being bought in Glasgow, and no doubt these imports were paid for by the exports.

During this period some changes in estate management were taking place It is a moot question whether the tenants on West Highland estates held tacks or leases of their holdings in early days. Some seannachies think that they did, but I am not aware that any tack is in existence of an earlier date than the seventeenth century. It is, however, certain that some tacks were granted at that period, but probably at that time the farms were not universally held on leases. Whereas there are scores of eighteenth century tacks in the Dunvegan Muniment Room, there are only two dated in the previous century, and only two are given in the history of the Clan Donald.

In all the seventeenth century tacks the duration of the lease is for the " life of the grantee, and the life of his eldest lauchful son, and for nineteen years after the death of his said son." In the eighteenth century the tacks only endured for a term of years, varying from nine to fifteen. It was then the custom that all the tacks should terminate at the same time, when the estate was again " sett " for another term of years.

The earliest of the four tacks to which I have referred was granted by Clanranald in 1625 " to the parson of Finnen." The extent of the farm is $4\frac{1}{2}$ marklands, a grassum is to be paid in four annual instalments of 1100 merks ; after this is paid, the rent is to be 40 merks. Besides the rent, the tenant and his successors are to " give thair personal service and presens to me and my airis in all our oasting, hunting, and convening, as all the remanent possessoris sall do and perform."

In 1626 a tack was granted by MacDonald of Sleat to Neil MacDonald of Boreray, in North Uist. The rent was to be £40 a year and 10 merks for teinds ; no grassum was payable, but a provision for service is inserted, " the said

Neil owand service to me by sea and land, as use and wont is."

This service was undoubtedly military service. The word " oasting " is hosting, that is, gathering the host of the clan together for war.

It should be noted that a grassum is a sum of money paid by a tenant when his lease is renewed.

In the two later tacks preserved at Dunvegan, the tack of Strond, in Harris, dated 1657, and the tack of Gesto, in Skye, dated 1674, this clause as to service is omitted. This marks the great change which had taken place in the condition of the country. On the mainland desperate clan battles continued to be fought up to almost the end of the seventeenth century. The last of these was the battle of Mulroy, between the Macdonalds of Keppoch and the Mackintoshes, in 1688, but in the Islands the last was the attack made in 1625 by several clans, acting under orders from the King, on the MacIans of Ardnamurchan.

In 1625 the possibility of attack by a hostile clan was still present in men's minds, and this provision was inserted in the tack. By 1657 it had passed away. " Oasting " might still be necessary to raise men to fight for the Kings of the house of Stuart, but the existence of a clan no longer depended on it, and the devoted loyalty of the clansmen to the King made any such provision superfluous, so it was omitted. In one later tack, however, which is dated 1707, Clanranald, after reciting the terms on which certain lands were let to his bard, McVurich, says :—" I also oblige me and my heirs to warrand the said lands to any one of his heirs, who shall be capable of serving in the station and office he now serves me in, of bard and seannachie." Whether the tenants on West Highland estates had ever in earlier times held tacks of their farms or not, they had never, as I believe, been called tacksmen. They now became known by that name, but, beyond the fact that their name was altered, there was no change in the position they occupied.

They still held the same farms on which their forbears had been settled from time immemorial. It is likely that some of the onerous services, which they had previously rendered to their Chiefs, gradually ceased to be demanded. They were no longer expected to attend on him as gentlemen in waiting, to give him and his numerous train of followers unlimited hospitality, or to receive as guests any sorners whom he might choose to quarter on them; but in other respects things went on as they had done before until after the '45. Whether military service was stipulated for in their tacks or not, the tacksmen still continued to render it; they still commanded their people in war, and governed them in peace. In a word, they still remained far more than tenants, as we understand the word.

The eldest son of a tacksman almost invariably succeeded his father. As I have pointed out, it was frequently provided for in the tack that he should do so. In early days the younger sons had generally remained at home. When the clan feuds were raging their services as leaders of the fighting force of the clan were all-important, but when these ceased, it is probable that an increasing number of the young men of this class went abroad, and took service under foreign potentates. Some, at all events, joined Mackay's Regiment, and went to Sweden, and there were many Highlanders engaged in the wars in Germany.

In the Dunvegan rent roll of the Skye estate, dated 1664, twenty-four farms appear as being held by 104 small tenants. I think it is probable that these were the farms which the Chief had originally kept in his own hands, and which had been cultivated for him by his own immediate dependents. I surmise that, at some period before 1664, he had ceased to keep any land in his own hands, and had divided these farms amongst the men who had formerly worked them for him, thus creating a new class of tenants, a class which we know at the present day as crofters.

But a reference to the rental shows that these small holdings were much larger than the crofts are now. Taking the merk in those days as roughly equivalent to the pound sterling of to-day, two or three are rented at £45, though some are as low as £11. The average is about £20, and these sums do not include the additional rent paid in kind. Probably these holdings have been sub-divided in later times. This, I believe, is the real origin of the crofting system.

But these changes were trivial. Down to the middle of the eighteenth century the clan system was still in full force, alike for purposes of peace and war. The Chief, assisted by the tacksmen, still continued to rule over his people. I find several instances, which show that they did so, in letters from Sir Alexander Macdonald. In 1743, he writes that a man from the MacLeod estate had come over into his country in order to court a girl, that a quarrel had arisen between the MacLeod and a MacDonald rival, and that the former had cut off the ears of the latter. Sir Alexander asks MacLeod to punish the delinquent. In another, dated March 1744, Sir Alexander tells how there has been " a small invasion from Knoydart," and how three cows had been carried off. He describes the steps which he is taking to recover the cattle, and to punish the offenders. And it was not only in small matters that they exercised this authority. Tradition says that a man was hanged at Dunvegan for murder in the year 1728 by the order of the Chief.

Between 1625 and 1745 the Western clans were only occasionally engaged on active service, but they still continued to be organised for military purposes. No doubt, many changes had taken place. Gradually the clans ceased to be naval powers, and no longer possessed fleets of birlinns; muskets began to be used instead of bows and arrows; defensive armour was no longer worn, and it is probable that the smaller claymore was the weapon employed instead the great two-handed broadsword, with which the clansmen had been previously armed.

It is possible that the very strenuous military training which I described in Chapter IV. may have been somewhat relaxed when the clan feuds came to an end, and the very existence of a clan no longer depended on its efficiency for war ; but to a very great extent it must have been maintained. The Highlanders who fought at Prestonpans, Falkirk, and Culloden showed no falling off, either in valour or efficiency, from the high standard as fighting men to which their fathers had attained, and up to 1745 the supply of arms must have been a matter of great importance, and the training of a clan's manhood in their use a duty which could not be neglected.

But after 1745 the whole system was entirely changed. The English Government had been greatly alarmed by the measure of success which the Highland army under the Prince had attained, and drastic measures were taken, which were calculated to make it impossible that such a thing should ever happen again. These I shall briefly describe.

Many Highland properties were confiscated on account of the share their owners had taken in the rising. These estates were not sold, but vested in the hands of commissioners, who used the profits for purposes of public utility. Large grants were made from these funds for making roads in the Highlands. One might have expected that these forfeitures would have had a great permanent effect on the ownership of land in the West Highlands, but, except in a very few cases they did not do so, for these estates were restored to the owners, or to their descendants, before many years had elapsed. Clan Ranald recovered his estate about 1770. In his attainder he had been called Donald MacDonald, whereas his real name was Ranald. Thus his attainder was void. General Fraser received a grant of the Lovat estates in 1774. Lochiel recovered his in 1784 under the general Act of amnesty.

In the interval, however, though their clansmen made most self-sacrificing efforts to help them, and though the French Government did something to assist, the exiled Chiefs were in a state of great poverty, and endured terrible hardships.

Other measures taken by the Government were more permanent in their results. In 1746 the Disarming Act was passed. By this Act the Highlanders were forbidden to possess any arms, and all those which they had were seized and taken away; the military service which the tenants had previously rendered to their Chiefs was no longer to be paid, and the " oasting, hunting, and convening," stipulated for in the tack of 1625, were made illegal. Thus the military side of the clan system was entirely destroyed.

To this Act was added yet another clause—" No man or boy shall, on any pretence whatsoever, wear or put on the clothes, commonly called the Highland clothes, that is to say, the plaid, phillabeg, or little kilt, trousers, shoulder belts, or any part whatsoever of what peculiarly belongs to the Highland garb, and no tartan, or party coloured plaid, shall be used for great coats, or upper coats." The Act came into force on August 1, 1748.

A great many people at the time thought that this was a very harsh and severe measure, for which there was no real necessity. The Lord President Forbes was one of them. In a letter to Brodie of Brodie, he expressed a very strong opinion on the subject ; but he did not succeed in his attempts to get the Bill modified.

The results of this measure were most far-reaching and important. While a clan remained a military organisation, the energies of its men were devoted to war, or to preparation for war. After the passing of this Act, their main occupation in life was taken away, and from this time dates the difficulty of finding employment for the Highlanders in their own country.

In the following year an Act was passed which brought to an end the clan system on its civil side. "The heritable jurisdictions," which the Chiefs had hitherto possessed and used, were taken away, and henceforth the people were governed under the laws of the realm. The administration of justice was put into the hands of Sheriff-Substitutes, who were then appointed all over Scotland. What we should call local government was exercised by the Justices of the Peace. From the minutes of a meeting held at Sconser in 1788 we get an idea of what matters they dealt with, and the methods they employed. Attendance at the meetings was compulsory, and absentees were fined ; they were the Highway Authority for Skye ; they made provision for the hiring of servants, and fixed the wages which were to be paid ; no one was allowed to pay more than the amount fixed. They made rules about such things as the maintenance of march dykes, the pounding of strayed sheep and cattle, the certificates of beggars, the liability of people keeping dangerous beasts for any damage, the use of properly stamped weights and measures. There are provisions that no man shall be intoxicated at a funeral, or attend without an invitation, and that no one shall leave Skye during harvest time without the leave of two Justices of the Peace. This leave the Justices are not to give until they have tried to get the applicant work in the island.

In theory the changes made by the Act of 1747 were very great. In practice they were probably small. The same people, who had previously acted under the authority of the Chief, were now Justices of the Peace acting under the authority of the King, and they probably carried out their duties in much the same way as before.

Thus the Clan system was completely destroyed. The Chiefs, who had been all-poweerful, became no more than the owners of large estates ; the Chieftains, who had ruled over their people for centuries, became mere tenant-farmers ; the clansmen, whose pride it had been that they belonged to a gallant and well-disciplined fighting force, became no more than peasants, whose occupation in life had been taken away, and whose national dress had been declared illegal.

There was only one thing which no Act of Parliament could destroy, and that was the devotion of the people to their Chiefs. There is ample evidence that this feeling of personal regard and affection lived on in spite of the Act ; indeed, to some extent it made the ordinance of Parliament a dead letter, for the people continued to obey the Chiefs, not because they were obliged to do so, but because they loved them. It is on record that many clansmen paid their rents twice over, once to the Commissioners for forfeited estates, and once to their beloved Chiefs, who were in exile. In an earlier chapter I described the self-sacrificing devotion of the clansmen on the MacLeod Estate to their Chief in the year 1777. Many other instances of the warm affection with which his people continued to regard a Chief might be cited, and, as I said in an earlier chapter, it is by no means dead amongst clansmen at the present day.

Up to about the year 1770, the old tacksmen remained on their farms, and still continued to work them on the patriarchal principle. They gave their servants no wages, but they regarded them as members of their families, and recognised that it was their duty to support them, whether they could find any work for them to do or not, though the difficulty of employing all the people was constantly becoming greater.

But about 1770 the old tacksmen began to emigrate, and leave the Highlands. At that time a great increase in rents was taking place all over the country. Prices were rising very rapidly, and probably, if the value of farm produce is taken into consideration, the new rents were not more burdensome than the old ones had been. But many of the farmers thought that it would be impossible to pay these higher rents.

The tacksmen on Lord Macdonald's estate formed a sort of company, bought 100,000 acres of land in South Carolina, and emigrated in a body, taking many of their people with them. On other estates considerable numbers of tacksmen left the country. The exodus, which began about 1770, continued during the next 40 or 50 years, until few of the old class of tacksmen remained on their farms, and their places were taken by men from other parts of Scotland.

This change killed the patriarchal system. The new tenants were bound to the people on their farms by no ties of blood, or of long standing affection. Farming had become a business based on commercial considerations. The farmers employed the men whose services they required, and paid them wages, but it was no business of theirs to support people merely because they lived on their farms.

Fortunately, as will appear in the next chapter, during the next fifty on sixty years, there was a good deal of employment for the people in the country, but they had lost one most important asset—they were no longer certain that, whether work could be found for them to do or not, they would be maintained by their superiors.

They also lost masters who, I am convinced, had been uniformly kind to them. The author of a report, which was rendered to the British Fishery Society about the state of affairs at Stein towards the end of the eighteenth century, says that the tacksmen had been " most tyrannical and cruel in dealing with their people." This may have been true in isolated cases, but I do not believe that it was generally true. When, in 1772 and 1811, some of the tacksmen proposed to emigrate and take their dependants with them, it seems incredible that people who had been so cruelly treated should be willing to accompany their tyrants when they went away. They certainly were willing to do so, and, in a good many cases, they actually did so.

By the time this report was written a good many new tenants were settled in the country, and I think it likely that, if any of the farmers had been cruel to their dependants, it was among the new-comers, and not among the old tacksmen, that this cruelty was found.

The passing away of the patriarchal system brought about another change in the conditions under which the people lived. The family ceased to be a self-sufficing unit in a clan. The workers, having become the whole-time servants of their masters, had less leisure in which to work for themselves, and having money, or the equivalent of money, they were able to pay others to do the work for them, which they had formerly done for themselves.

As time went on labour began to be specialised. Weavers, tailors, shoemakers, and other tradesmen were found in every township, and, finally, though not for a long time, shops were opened, at which the people could buy the goods which they had formerly made for themselves.

Thus, before the dawn of the 19th century, the clan and the patriarchal systems had been entirely destroyed, the conditions of life in the West Highlands had been completely altered, and " the old order had passed away, giving place to the new."

CHAPTER VIII.

EMPLOYMENT AND UNEMPLOYMENT.

WAGES—KELP—SERVICE IN ARMY—FISHING, GROWING
ROOTS—TEMPORARY WORK, ROAD MAKING—UN
WONTED COMFORTS — CONSUMPTION OF WHISKY—
SHEEP DISPLACE CATTLE—LAND GOES OUT OF CUL-
TIVATION—PEACE DECREASES DEMAND OF MEN FOR
THE ARMY—FAILURE OF KELP INDUSTRY—CONDI-
TION OF THE PEOPLE—THE CLEARANCES—THE
POTATO FAMINE.

After the changes described in the last chapter had taken place, though some of the people had crofts, most of them depended on finding some work to do, by which they could earn their daily bread. Down to the end of the eighteenth century the people still had all the employments open to them which were described in Chapter IV., the only difference being that, whereas in earlier days they had received in return for their labour the maintenance of themselves and their families, they were now being paid wages. Fortunately, we know what wages workers were then receiving, as these were fixed at a meeting of Magistrates, held at Sconser, in Skye, in 1788. Farm servants were divided into two classes—

(1) Competent agricultural labourers ;
(2) Striplings and less skilled men.

Men in Class 1 received £2 a year, and 4 pairs of shoes. Men in Class 2 received £1 a year, and 4 pairs of shoes. Herdsmen in Class 1 received 5 pairs of shoes. Shoes were valued at 2s 6d a pair.

If a man wished to have grazing for a cow, the following sums were deducted from his wages :—

For a cow, £1.
For a yeld beast, 10s.
For a two-year-old beast, 8s.
For a stirk, 5s.

Common women servants received 8s a year and 2 pairs of shoes. Dairywomen received 15s, and 3 pairs of shoes. Servants are not to be given warm milk. Probably this means they were to be given skimmed milk.

Men engaged for the harvest received 8s, and no shoes. Their work began on the day the corn was cut, and ended on the day it was stacked. All these classes of servants received board and lodging, as well as their wages. Casual labourers, engaged by the day " at their own charges," were paid 8d a day.

No master was allowed to pay higher wages than those fixed. All servants must behave " mannerly and obediently " to their masters. Servants, not engaged for a fixed time, must give 40 days' notice before they leave. As the purchasing price of money was then about $5\frac{1}{2}$ times what it is now, the wages were really much higher than they seem to us to have been. When, however, we speak of wages, we must remember that these were largely, probably entirely, paid in kind—in meal, wool, a cow's grass, possibly in weddens. There was very little money in the country. There were no shops, and, even if a man had received his wages in cash, he would have found it very difficult to obtain what he wanted for his money. At that time the laird's factor used to charter ships, which brought such articles as tea, sugar, wine, brandy, and tobacco, and these he used to sell to those who could afford to buy them.

During the eighteenth century several new employments opened to the people, which greatly improved the amenities of their lives.

I. Early in the eighteenth century it had been discovered that the seaweed which grew on the rocks, and, to a still greater extent, the floating ware cast up by the sea, were rich in alkalis and iodine. I took the following account of how kelp is made from an article which appeared in the " Oban Times " some time ago.

The former, which is called " beach wrack," and grows in great quantities on the eastern shores of the Long Island, contains iodine. The latter, which is known as " tangle,"

and is found on the western shores of the Islands, produces
soda and potash. The collection of the " tangle," and the
cutting of the " beach wrack " involved much labour, and took
a long time. Each year, some time in June, the people
engaged in the industry migrated to sheilings, built in con-
venient places on the sea-shore and in these they lived for
six weeks or two months, while the work was in progress.
The first job to be done on arrival was to repair the sheilings,
and make them fairly comfortable abodes during the coming
weeks. Then the work began.

At low tide the drift weed was collected, or the growing
weed cut. The latter operation could only be carried out
in the same place once in three years, as the sea ware, after
being cut, took that length of time to grow, before it would
yield a full crop on a further cutting.

The weed, which had been collected or cut, was piled
in great heaps upon the shore. Round these heaps long ropes,
made of heather, were bound to prevent the ware from
floating out to sea as the tide rose. The two ends of the rope
were fastened on the shore, and, when the tide was high, the
floating piles of " tangle " or " wrack " were drawn to land.

The weed was then spread out to dry on the grass ; it
was turned over from time to time, and treated in much the
same way as hay. This took some time, and its successful
drying depended, to a great extent, on the weather. While
the weed was drying, " athan," or " kilns," were dug in the
ground. Each of these was from 12 to 24 feet long, 2 feet
broad, and $2\frac{1}{2}$ feet deep, and would contain enough weed to
make about a ton of kelp.

When the weed was dry, some burning straw or heather
was placed at the bottom of the kiln, and the weed was piled
on the top. It was considered necessary that the burning
of the weed should be slow, and, while it was going on, the
kilns were watched. If any flames appeared this indicated
that the process was going on too quickly, and, in order to
slow it down, more weed was flung on the kiln. The burning
took some time, and was continued till the weed ran into a
kind of slag. This was collected, and sent South by sea,
generally to Liverpoool, to be refined and further treated.

Kelp was already being made in the Orkneys in 1722, but the industry was not introduced into the Western Isles till a few years later. In 1735 the work began in South Uist, and in 1748 in Harris. Here the results were very soon seen in the increased revenue derived from the island. In 1744 Harris was worth £356, in 1754 it had risen to £544, and in 1769 to £806. In Glenelg, where there was no kelp, values rose at the same time, but not to the same extent. The value of Glenelg in 1744 was £373 ; in 1754, £407 ; in 1769, £679. The development of this industry between 1750 and 1820 was amazing. At one time kelp was worth £22 a ton. This was not maintained for long, but the average price during the first twenty years of the nineteenth century was £10 10s.

At this period the kelp was a source of great prosperity in the Long Island, whence between 6000 and 7000 tons were exported annually, bringing in a revenue of £60,000 to £70,000 to the islands. Owing to the fact that much less floating sea ware is cast up in Skye, the magnitude of the industry there was insignificant compared with that in the Long Island. In 1819, 91 tons were exported to Liverpool from Lochs Dunvegan and Bracadale. The gross value was only about £800, but, though this was a small sum compared to the revenues derived from kelp in the Long Island, it was not to be despised.

The industry brought great wealth to the lairds, specially to those whose property was in the Long Island. It was also an enormous advantage to the people. The cost of manufacturing the kelp was about £2 10s a ton, and all this went into the pockets of the workers. I have not been able to ascertain whether they were paid by time wages or by piece-work.

II. During the last half of the eighteenth century large numbers of men were raised in the Highlands for the army, carrying out the policy which had been originally suggested by President Forbes, and which was adopted by Pitt. Without careful research into the military history of the times, it would be difficult to say how many Highland regiments were embodied during this period. A battalion was raised to meet some special emergency, disbanded when that emergency had passed away, and re-embodied when a fresh crisis arose.

Often the names and numbers of regiments were changed, so
the records are very confusing. But it is a certain fact that
many thousands of men from the West Highlands were
fighting with splendid courage and devotion in all parts of
the world, during the long series of wars, which lasted, with
short intervals of peace, from 1760 to 1815. All through this
time the calls on the manhood of the country were incessant.
An army on active service must always suffer heavy losses.
These become heavier still when it is operating in a hot and
unhealthy climate. A letter, written by the officer command-
ing the Second Battalion of the Black Watch in 1786, is still
in existence. This letter indicates that, of the men who had
originally belonged to the battalion when it came to India
in 1781, only enough to form one conpany were left. Five
years of active service had accounted for the rest, and their
places had been filled by fresh drafts.

These facts are sufficient to show what an enormous
amount of employment the army offered to the Highlanders,
and what magnificent services they rendered to King and
Country in a time of dire need.

III. About the year 1790, the British Fishery Society
founded a fishing village at Stein, in Skye; provided boats, nets,
lines, and all that is necessary for the prosecution of the
industry, and every effort was made to induce the West
Highlanders to pursue fishing as the business of their lives.
From the reports of the Society it appears that this effort
met with little success.

No doubt from the earliest times the Highlanders had
done some desultory fishing, but they had never done more.
In the time of Charles I. fishing was being vigorously prosecuted on the West Coast of Scotland, but the fishermen were
Englishmen and Dutchmen, not native Highlanders. In the
report on Harris, already referred to, which was dated 1772,
the author says that " enormous shoals of herring regularly
visit the coast of the island, and cod and ling are very plentiful,
but practically nothing is done to catch them."

At the present day a few West Highlanders are earning
their living by fishing, and a great many more fish occasionally,
but the important fishing industry, which is being prosecuted

on our western shores, is being carried on by boats which come from the East Coast, and the effort to make the West Highlanders fishermen may be said to have failed. It is certain that they have not made a great and profitable industry of fishing as the Bretons, the Lofoten Islanders, and the people on the east coast of England and Scotland have done, and it is equally certain that the opportunity of doing so has not been lacking.

Why have they not done so ? The author of an interesting report on the proceedings of the British Fishery Society at Stein thinks this failure was caused by the remains of the feudal system, to which he traces every evil he perceives, Under this thrice-accursed system, he says, fighting was the only honourable occupation for men. In the intervals of peace they might, he adds, condescend to do a little work on the cultivation of the soil, but they looked on fishing as an ignoble trade, only fit for the deformed and the weakling. He does not explain how deformed weaklings are going to face the hardships and bear the toil of a fisherman's life.

He goes on to suggest that the best way to make the people fish would be to take away their crofts, and in this way compel them to turn to fishing for a livelihood. Here I think he probably hits the real reason why Highlanders have never taken seriously to fishing. The industry is one to which a man must dedicate his whole life ; it is not one which can be treated as supplementary to another. While the Highlanders retained their crofts they looked on the cultivation of them as the main business of their lives, and regarded fishing as a merely occasional occupation, which might be pursued when leisure permitted.

It is most unfortunate that they took that view. A small croft, at the best, can only provide its owner with a very poor livelihood. A fisherman, though his life is an arduous one, can earn a fair living. It is probably the attempt to combine the two trades which has prevented the one, which might have made the Highlanders happy and prosperous, from being prosecuted with the energy and zeal, which alone could make it a success.

Possibly the amount of employment, which was being offered to the people in other and more congenial directions, may have had something to do with the failure to engage them in the fishing industry.

IV. For centuries the live stock in the Islands had been insufficiently fed in winter. Somewhere about 1760 the attention of the Society for Propagating Christian Knowledge in Scotland was called to this, and they devoted part of a legacy of £2000, which had been left them by a Mr Wood, to offering premiums for raising clover and other artificial grasses for hay, with the humane idea of mininising the sufferings of the cattle in the winter.

In the regulations of the Dunvegan Estate, dated 1769, it is provided that each tenant shall sow a certain quantity both of grass seeds and of turnips every year for wintering, and prizes of £5 are offered to the tenant who grows the best crops. This caused a great many farmers to start growing these crops, and a considerable increase in the amount of labour required on the farms.

V. The prosperity brought by the kelp industry indirectly greatly benefited the people. The lairds, enriched by the large profits from kelp, were restoring old castles, or building new mansion houses, planting woods, and making all sorts of improvements on their estates, and this gave much employment to the humbler classes.

Between 1770 and 1820 there was much work being done of a temporary description, which, however, went on for a good many years, and was of inestimable value to the people. Kail-yards and arable fields were being fenced, march dykes between the farms were being put up, and a great deal of land was being drained. As the new tenants came in, they required better houses than those with which the old tacksmen had been content. So that building operations called for an immense amount of labour.

VI. More important than any of these was the work which was being done on the highways. The improvement of the roads was at that period engaging the attention of people in all parts of the country. They certainly needed it. Even in the neighbourhood of London a few years earlier they had been in a shocking condition. Vanbrugh, describing the adventures of a newly-elected M.P. on his way to London, says :—" All the exertions of six horses, two of which had been taken from the plough, could not save the family coach from being embedded in a quagmire." A little earlier, Prince George of Denmark, travelling to Petworth, had only been able to come nine miles in six hours. If this was the case near London, we need not wonder that the remote islands of the West were almost completely cut off from the outer world in the 18th century.

It is difficult for us in these days to imagine the isolation in which our forefathers lived. In the early years of the century there was no post office in Skye, neither were there any mails. There was an official at Dunvegan called " Macleod's post." It was his duty to take " expresses " to any place to which he was sent. He received a regular wage of fifteen shillings a year, and fifteen shillings for a journey to Edinburgh. This seems very little, but it was equivalent to £9 in our own days.

As early as 1742 MacLeod says in a letter that he will write again by the next post, from which I assume that a mail was then being sent to the Western Isles. But the only post office in Skye was at Dunvegan, and people, who lived in all parts of the island, had to send there for their letters. The authorities would not allow a bag to be dropped by the postman at Sconser, and in 1753 Lady Margaret MacDonald wrote several letters, bitterly complaining of this, and asking that a post office should be opened either at Portree or Sconser.

The outer islands were served by a packet which sailed from Dunvegan once a fortnight. Stornoway had a fortnightly packet sailing from Poolewe.

In Skye there were a few old roads of a somewhat primitive description. All able-bodied men were bound to give six days' labour every year on the roads. At the meeting of Magistrates in 1788, already referred to, each gentleman tacksman was to furnish a list of all such within his bounds, but it was provided that in future labour should be commuted for two shillings and sixpence a head, and that tacksmen should pay twopence in the pound on their rent in lieu of their personal attendance.

This was probably the first germ of the system of rates in the Highlands. Poor rates, school rates, County Assessments were all unknown. Local government was certainly cheap in those days, and I believe it was also effective.

Though a highway committee was appointed in 1788, and instructed to obtain the services of a contractor to carry out the proposed schemes, very little was done for some years. But after the beginning of the 19th century, the making of roads was being vigorously pushed forward. About 1805, the Commissioners for Highland Roads and Bridges, acting with the county authorities, turned their attention to Skye. A road was planned from Stein to Sconser, which was estimated to cost £6433. This was afterwards increased to £10,746. About 1814, Telford, the famous engineer, was called in, and he pronounced even the second estimate to be entirely inadequate. The actual cost of this road was somewhere about £40,000. The Commissioners found half the money required out of the proceeds of estates which had been forfeited after the '45 ; the tenants paid an amount of road money in addition to their rents, which amounted to about £2100 ; the crofters gave some labour free of charge ; and the owners of the land gave £15,000. Besides the main arteries of communication, many small local highways were made, and the expenditure on roads and bridges throughout the country must have been very large. No doubt the same work was being pushed forward all over the West Highlands.

In all these different ways the people certainly had more work to do than they ever had before, or than they have ever had since. Seeing that a sufficiency of employment is the greatest blessing which a community can possess, this period was a very prosperous one in the history of the West Highlanders, specially in the Long Island, where the kelp industry was in such a flourishing condition.

This period of prosperity brought about some changes in the habits of the people, which deserve to be noticed. To some extent the people began to use such articles as tea, tobacco, and other imported luxuries, but only, I think, when such goods were smuggled into the country. Duties were then very high. About 1740, tea, which had paid duty, cost 28s a pound, sugar 4s a pound. Some old accounts show that even the wealthier classes bought tea by the ounce, and only used it very occasionally. About 1780 tea cost 6s a pound, and sugar 1s. These prices were far beyond the means of the poorer classes, and, even had they possessed the money, it would have been difficult to get the goods.

It is also probable that at this time a good deal of whisky began to be distilled and drunk. In a previous chapter I expressed the opinion that, in early days, whatever the lairds and tacksmen may have been, the masses of the people were very abstemious, and that, as Martin says, " their drink was water." But in Badenoch, according to Miss Grant, considerable quantities of whisky were being consumed at this time, specially at funerals and weddings, and I think it probable that, during this period, in the Western Isles also whisky became the drink of the people.

To supply these newly-felt needs many illicit stills were working all over the Highlands, and in so wild and desolate a country the Revenue officers found it very difficult to discover the stills. Many vessels also were engaged in smuggling dutiable goods into the Islands, and, such was the courage and address of these skippers, they more often than not succeeded in eluding the cruisers which were trying to capture them.

An old story relates that on one occasion a Revenue cutter in chase of a smuggler succeeded in driving her into Loch Dunvegan. The officer in command of the cutter fancied that he had his prize safe in the land-locked waters of the bay. But between the northern end of the island which lies in the mouth of the loch and the promontory of Fiochaid, there is a passage, through which a small vessel can reach the open sea. It is full of rocks, and only a man who knows the channel can venture into it. To the amazement and disgust of the Revenue officer, the smuggling skipper, who knew every rock on the coast, made for this passage and effected his escape, while the King's officer, who was not so well informed, did not dare to follow him.

The Customs and Excise duties being at this time very high, both the illicit stills on shore and the smugglers at sea flourished exceedingly. It appears that the smuggled goods found their way, not only into the houses of the poor, but into the homes of the wealthier classes. A meeting of Magistrates was held at Portree on August 15, 1744, to concert plans for suppressing the " fair trade." From the minutes of this meeting it appears that all the Magistrates were able to do was to solemnly promise that they would abstain from drinking smuggled tea themselves, and, " if it was humanly possible, to restrain their wives and daughters from doing so," but they appear to have been very doubtful whether it would be " humanly possible " to do this.

Unhappily, during the first 30 years of the 19th century, all these sources of employment were dried up. First, the work available on the farms was much diminished. The cattle were removed, and sheep became the principal stock on the land. I have not been able to fix the exact date when this change began to be made, but it is probably safe to say that it was being carried out during the first 20 years of the century.

In some letters written in 1771 I find the substitution of sheep for cattle suggested because in that year a most destructive cattle plague had broken out. The writer describes, in the darkest possible terms, the miserable condition to which all classes in the community had been reduced, and thought that any change, which would minimise the chance of such a disaster recurring in the future, must be a change for the better. Some of the older ones among them may have remembered that the same thing had happened in 1717.

This reason for making the change may have been in the minds of some of the lairds and tacksmen who carried it into effect, but I am under the impression that other considerations weighed much more heavily with all the parties concerned. Elaborate estimates had been drawn up. In these were clearly shown the amount of capital required to stock land with sheep or with cattle, the working expenses which must be incurred when the different kinds of stock were on the ground, and the profits which might be expected under the two systems. These figures convinced the landowners and the tacksmen that sheep farming would be infinitely more profitable than cattle farming had ever been. Consequently, about the year 1811, on many estates tenants were found ready to offer three times the amount of rent previously paid, and, in the same year, the purchaser of Glenelg was willing to give a sum amounting to 50 years' purchase of the net rental in 1810.

It was soon found, however, that in these estimates several important factors had been left out of account, and some serious drawbacks not realised or foreseen. These I briefly summarise.

(1) If cattle are liable to occasional outbreaks of cattle plague, sheep are subject to the mysterious and constantly recurring disease called braxy, and the death-rate from braxy on some farms is very high. It attacks sheep very suddenly, and kills them very quickly. So far, no preventive of the disease has been discovered, though inoculation has been tried with some measure of success.

(2) For some unknown reason the death-rate from braxy is higher among home-wintered sheep than among sheep wintered in the low country. For this reason, though excellent crops of roots can be grown in the West Highlands, farmers send a great many sheep to be wintered in the South at a very heavy cost.

(3) It is found that when strange sheep are put on any given farm, large numbers of them die until they get acclimatised. Thus the first tenants who introduced sheep suffered very considerable loss. To recoup them for this loss, a system was devised under which an outgoing tenant receives a price for his stock largely in excess of its market value. This means that the amount of capital required to stock a sheep farm is considerably increased, and high capitalisation is always a drawback to any industry.

(4) Many farms in the Islands are bounded on one side, sometimes even on two or three sides, by lofty precipices, which rise hundreds of feet above the sea. On these are many ledges covered with soil on which the rich grass fed

9

by the salt spray, which sheep love, freely grows. Cattle rarely fall over these precipices, but sheep frequently jump down on a ledge a little below the summit, attracted by the sweet pasture growing upon it. Unless a shepherd comes by and rescues him, that sheep's fate is sealed. He soon consumes all the grass on the ledge, he cannot jump back, and he finally dies of starvation, and falls into the sea. This is called the " black death," and causes immense losses on many farms.

(5) On many hillsides in the West Highlands the soil is so poor that it produces nothing but rough bent grass. Cattle will eat this grass, and thrive upon it. Sheep will not touch it. Therefore an enormous quantity of grass, which had previously been utilised, was wasted. Some compensation was found for this loss in another direction, which had been foreseen, and made the most of, as an argument in favour of the change of system. Sheep were able to get at and consume grass growing in numerous and remote corries among the mountains, which cattle had been unable to reach. But probably the loss was much greater than the gain.

(6) There can be no doubt that cattle manure land better than sheep do. As I have before remarked, Dean Monro gives glowing accounts concerning the fertility of many islands in the Hebrides, which a modern farmer would scarcely endorse, and it is quite possible that, during the last hundred years, the soil has become less productive than it was in the old days when cattle were on the ground. I do not suppose that it is possible to arrive at any definite conclusion as to whether this is really the case or not.

(7) The plague of bracken which now covers so many once fertile hillsides in the country may be due to the introduction of sheep. It is extremely probable that they carry the seed in their wool, and so spread the bracken broadcast.

The effects of these drawbacks soon began to be felt. In 1825 the rents fixed in 1811 had to be reduced by nearly 50 per cent., and about the same time the purchaser of Glenelg re-sold the property for a much smaller sum than he had given. The fall may have been partly due to the economic condition into which the country had fallen after the peace of 1815, but the fact that no important recovery took place till about 1860 strengthens my opinion that it was mainly due to the causes I have mentioned.

The question whether the change from cattle to sheep was financially a success or a failure is a very difficult one to answer. On the one hand, in 1825 rents were still double what they had been in 1810 ; on the other hand, they would certainly have risen in 1811, even if the cattle had remained on the land, but we have no idea what the amount of that rise would have been. I rather incline to the opinion that it has made very little difference, but if I am right in the last two reasons I have given, the introduction of sheep may have done a great deal of mischief.

Whether the substitution of sheep for cattle was economically a wise measure or not, to the masses of the people it was a great misfortune. Some landowners foresaw that it would be so, and to their honour be it said, refused to sanction a change which, though it might be favourable to themselves, would do an injury to their clansmen. The harm done to the working classes was both material and sentimental. It was material because it decreased the amount of available employment on the farms, it was sentimental because it destroyed old customs and habits which had been practised for centuries.

A few shepherds can attend to great numbers of sheep, and, even when the sheep are being clipped, only a small number of men are required. On the other hand, it is quite certain that the care of the cattle, the milking of the cows morning and evening, and the making of butter and cheese, had given the people a great deal of employment. This was now lost.

And this was not all. The cattle had been the main object of interest in their lives. The summer migrations to the shielings had been delightful holidays. They varied the monotony of life. They were eagerly looked forward to for months before they took place, and they filled the winters which followed with pleasant recollections. The material loss to the people was bad enough, but the feeling that the centre of their lives had been knocked out was much worse.

That feeling was strong at the time, and it remains even to the present day. Not very long ago I met an old fisherman at Mallaig. He told me that his parents had lived in Skye. He dwelt upon the happy lives they had lived in the old days when the island was full of black cattle, and a hundred years after they had been removed, he was still deploring their loss.

It is difficult to exaggerate the magnitude of the misfortune which fell on the masses of the people in the West Highlands when sheep took the place of cattle as the main stock on the land.

About the same time much of the land, on which cereals had been grown from time immemorial, went out of cultivation, and this was a hardly less serious blow to the people, for yet another source of employment was dried up. This was not due, as is often supposed, to a decrease in population ; neither was it caused by the crofters diminishing the amount of corn which they grew for their own use. The real reason was that the tacksmen ceased to grow corn because it no longer paid them to do so, and because it had ceased to be necessary.

Communications had improved, the conditions, which had made it so difficult at an earlier period to bring cereals from other parts of the country, had changed, and it was now possible to import corn at a cheaper rate than it could be grown at home. The natural consequence was that much land went out of cultivation. For the same reason a great deal of land in England during the last fifty years has been laid away to grass, with the same unfortunate results to the agricultural labourers.

This change, however, was inevitable. It is impossible in the West Highland climate and on West Highland soil to grow corn which can compete, either in quality or price, with that grown in the more favoured South.

In 1815 the Napoleonic wars came to an end. To the nation at large this was a great blessing ; to the West Highlanders it was a great misfortune. For more than sixty years vast numbers of them had found the employment, which was more congenial to them than any other, in the army, and they had covered themselves with glory in scores of arduous campaigns. Now regiments were disbanded, the call for men to fill up the ranks which had been depleted by heavy losses ceased, and thousands of men came home to compete for work in the already congested labour market. No doubt some West Highlanders continued to serve under the colours, but the number was greatly reduced, and few of us now realise what a crushing blow to our countrymen the peace of 1815 really was.

Between 1826 and 1828 came an utterly unexpected disaster in the collapse of the kelp industry.

From 1819 to 1826 the average price per ton at					
Liverpool was	...	...	...	...	£8 0 0
Deduct cost of manufacture	...	£2 10 0			
Freight to Liverpool	...	...	0 13 0		
Agent's charges ...	...	...	0 9 6		
					3 12 6
Profit per ton	...	...	...	...	£4 7 6
In 1828 the price at Liverpool was	...	...	£3 13 4		
Deductions as before, except that Agent's					
charges, being a percentage, were less	...	3 7 4			
Profit	...	...	...	...	£0 6 0

To some extent this may have been due to chemical discoveries, which provided substitutes for the alkali obtained from kelp, but it was mainly due to the removal of the duties on pot pearl, black ash, sulphur, and barilla. The kelp-owners petitioned the Government that the duties might be reimposed, but they petitioned in vain, and I believe that in 1830 the value of kelp at Liverpool was not much over £2, a price at which it was impossible to manufacture it.

One or two efforts were made to resuscitate the industry, which met with some temporary success, and a little kelp is still made in the Long Island, but it is hardly an exaggeration to say that about 1828 kelp ceased to be a source of profit to the Islanders. On all the islands this was a loss ; in the Long

Island it was a disaster, which reduced the people to a state of terrible poverty, and completely ruined some of the lairds. Now, in 1929, I understand there is some prospect of a revival in the industry.

Naturally the temporary work, which I referred to above, also ceased. The landlords, crippled by the loss of revenues derived from kelp, were no longer able to carry out improvements on their estates. By 1829 most of the roads were finished, most of the draining, planting and fencing was completed, and most of the new houses were built. The number of people who lost their employment at this time, and with it their means of living, was very large.

As, one after another, all these varied sources of employment were dried up, the condition of the West Highlanders became more and more pitiable. They were rapidly increasing in numbers (see Chapter III.). The old system, under which their maintenance had been guaranteed to them, had passed away for ever. Most of them were cottars, and occupied no land at all ; the holdings of those who had crofts were very small, and, in a great many cases, a crofter's relations had built themselves houses on his land, and five or six families were living on a single small holding.

A few shepherds and farm servants were still required. Some of the people found work in the households of the lairds and tacksmen ; the women earned something by knitting socks and stockings ; some men may have made their way to the South and found work there ; but, as steamers had not begun to run, this must have been very difficult. Sportsmen and tourists had not begun to bring money into the country, and probably the years between 1830 and 1850 were the saddest and the darkest through which the masses of the people in the West Highlands have ever passed.

Thinking men, who realised the conditions, were racking their brains to find some remedy for the evil. Efforts were again made to prosecute the fishing industry ; the making of bricks was inaugurated in Skye, where there was some clay ; one or two lairds bought small sailing vessels, and endeavoured to create some trade with foreign countries. Sir James Matheson carried out vast improvements in Lewis, giving a great deal of employment to his people, and similar efforts were made in other parts of the country. But all of them were only local and transitory, and the best friends of the humbler classes began, slowly and reluctantly, to realise that emigration on a large scale was the only real and permanent remedy for their troubles.

But the idea was not at all palatable to the people. Fifty years earlier they had been ready enough to accompany the gentlemen tacksmen, who were themselves leaving the old country, but it was one thing to go with c d and trusted friends who they knew would take care of them, and quite another thing to face a long voyage with no one to guide them to a distant land of which they knew nothing, where they had no friends, and where they would have to begin a new life amongst strangers, who did not speak their language. No wonder that they shrank from facing such an ordeal, and it became abundantly clear that they would not go willingly.

The owners of some estates in the West Highlands, rightly or wrongly, made up their minds that, as the people would not emigrate willingly, they were justified in compelling them to do so. These lairds evicted the people from their holdings, and forced them to seek new homes beyond the seas.

For doing this they have been denounced in very strong language. It has been said that their motives were purely selfish ones, and that they made these " clearances," as they were called, because they believed that their estates would yield higher rents if they were under sheep or deer than would be possible if they were in the hands of crofters.

There is ample evidence that some of the lairds were not actuated by such miserable and contemptible motives as these, that they were filled with pity for their unfortunate people, who were in such a state of acute suffering, and honestly believed that emigration was the only remedy by which their condition could be improved.

But, after all, it was only a few lairds who acted in this manner. The bulk of the people remained in their homes, and lived for another fifteen years under conditions which it

is very sad to contemplate. A competent observer, now long
since passed to her rest, told me that she had never heard of
any cases of actual starvation among them, and that they
were marvellously contented with their lot, hard though it
was. But they were desperately poor, they had lost the few
comforts which they had possessed in happier times, and seem
to have forgotten that they had ever enjoyed them.

The following story was told me by one of the people in
Skye. The wife of an island laird gave a pound of tea to the
wife of the joiner on her husband's estate about the year 1840.
The good lady called her friends together to partake of the
unwonted luxury. She soaked the tea leaves in hot water,
poured off the liquid, and gave her friends the tea leaves to
be eaten with a spoon.

In 1846 came the great and crowning disaster of the
potato famine. I have heard many accounts of this appalling
misfortune from the lips of people who were living in the
country at the time, and I have had access to a number of
letters and to many contemporary reports and newspaper
articles.

Only one who has studied such documents can realise
the magnitude of the disaster. It is no exaggeration to say
that during this awful time thousands of people were face
to face with starvation. In my History of the MacLeods I
have related at length the story of what the Chief of that clan
did to save his people, and I need not repeat it here. But his
efforts were only local, and no one man could cope with such
a tremendous disaster. Charitable funds were opened in
Glasgow and Edinburgh, and, before the end of the year
1849, over £210,000 had been raised and spent in relieving
the distress, which was so desperately acute all over the West
Highlands.

The most important result of the potato famine was that
something like half the population, forced by stern necessity,
emigrated, and, since then, the population of the West Highlands has been steadily falling. In 1845 the population of
Skye was estimated at 29,500 ; in 1881 it was 16,889 ; in 1911
it was 13,319 ; in 1921 it was 11,031. Since 1845 not very

far short of two-thirds of the population have left their homes. The only consolation is that they have done exceedingly well in the land of their adoption, and we must hope and trust that the measures, which the Government have adopted in recent years, will enable those who remain to do equally well in the land of their birth.

CHAPTER IX.

A WEST HIGHLAND ESTATE DURING FOUR CENTURIES.

SCOTS MONEY—MEASURES OF LAND, VALUE IN 1527, 1542,
1610—RENT ROLLS, CESS AND TEINDS ON CREDIT
SIDE, GROSS VALUES, 1527 TO 1881—REASONS FOR RISE
—BURDENS ON LAND, CESS, PAYMENTS TO CLERGY
—SCHOOLS, CHARITY, MANAGEMENT—PERCENTAGE
OF BURDENS TO GROSS VALUE.

In earlier chapters I have dealt with many subjects
which relate to the land. In Chapters II. and III. I discussed
the conditions under which it was owned by the Chiefs, and
occupied by the Chieftains, and in Chapter IV. I described
the methods of cultivating the soil which were employed in
ancient times, the crops which were grown on the arable
ground, and the live stock which found a home among the
hills.

In the present chapter I shall endeavour to obtain some
idea of the gross value of the land in the Islands at different
periods, and of the burdens which it had to bear.

Though most of my information is derived from papers
in the Dunvegan charter-chest, and applies to a single estate,
conditions were similar all over the country; and I believe
that the records of what happened on that one estate will
give an idea of what was taking place throughout the whole
of the Island Lord's dominions, and make clear to the reader's
mind the great changes which have brought the Highlands
to the condition in which we know them.

All the values in ancient documents are given in Scots
money. I shall reduce all these to equivalent values in
sterling money, but the following tables of the money, and of

the weights and measures, which were used in Scotland up to quite a late period, may be interesting :—

TABLE OF SCOTS MONEY.

		£	s.	d.				£	s.	d.
1 dozt.	=	0	0	$0\frac{2}{12}$	1 shilling	=	0	0	1
1 bodle	=	0	0	$0\frac{4}{12}$	1 merk	=	0	1	$1\frac{4}{12}$
1 plack	=	0	0	$0\frac{8}{12}$	1 pound	=	0	1	8

Up to 1720 the merk, and not the pound Scots, was generally the unit of value in the Highlands.

Meal was weighed by the trone measure. Of this I give a table :—

1½ pints	=	1 lippie.	4 pecks	......	1 firlot.
4 lippies	=	1 peck.	4 firlots	......	1 boll.

The boll weighed a little over 156 pounds, as against the boll of 140 lbs. now in use.

A boll of oats was the amount which would make a boll of meal, and is usually reckoned at 5 firlots.

The stones used in weighing butter and cheese were the trone stones, which weighed 24 lbs.

There can be no doubt that in very early days there were rentals in existence which indicated the value of the land in different districts, and it is probable that the officials, who drew up the charters which were granted to the Island Chiefs during the closing years of the 15th century, had these in their hands. The old rentals are lost, but many of the charters have been preserved, and from them we can obtain some idea of the value of land at an early period.

In these charters a given number of unciates are granted. An unciate is land the yearly rent of which is equivalent to one ounce of silver. This was valued at £2 13s 4d Scots, or 4s 5½d sterling money.

In Glenelg, which was granted to MacLeod at a much earlier date, the term davoch is used. *The Davoch in the Lowlands*=4 ploughgates, and 1 ploughgate=8 oxgangs, or 100 acres Scots. In the Highlands, MacBain says a davoch is land which will graze 60 cows, and Skene says it is the same as the unciate. It is sometimes called the tirunga, Gaelic for ounce land. The term is used in Glenelg, which contained 12 davochs. Here it is certainly equivalent to the unciate.

On this value of the unciate or davoch " the old valuation " is based. As the same values are given for Glenelg, which was granted in 1342, and for the Island estate, which were granted in 1498, it is probable that this old valuation had been in force for a long time. Probably early in the 16th century a " new valuation was made four times as great as the old one." In this the value of the unciate or davoch was £10 13s 4d Scots, or 17s 8½d sterling money. I think that probably the old valuation gives us the value of land about the middle of the 14th century, and the new valuation fixes its value in the early sixteenth century.

In these valuations due consideration was given to the fertility of the soil in the different islands. In fertile Islay there are only 1560 acres in the unciate, in Mull there are 4532 acres, in rugged Harris there are 6900 acres, in Skye, where the splendid but barren Coolins cover so much of the ground, there are 8224 acres. This makes it quite clear that the unciate was a measure of value, and not a measure of extent, and probably, whatever its value may have been at different periods, that value was approximately the same in all the islands.

As silver was weighed by troy weight, in which there are 20 dwt. to the ounce, an unciate, or davoch, of land was divided into 20 penny lands, each of which was worth, in the first valuations, 2s 8d Scots, 2⅔d sterling. It must be clearly understood that a penny land is not land worth a penny, but land worth the twentieth part of the sum an unciate is worth at any given time.

In some charters, in which smaller areas of land are granted, two other terms are used, the " pound land," which was worth £1 Scots, or 1s 8d sterling, and the merkland, which was worth 13s 4d Scots, or 1s 1⅓d sterling.

In Skye the valuation of farms is given in penny lands. In Islay the unit was the merkland, which contained five penny lands. For purposes of comparison I shall in all my calculations employ the merkland as the unit, dividing the unciates by 4, and multiplying the penny lands by five.

The earliest record of actual values, which I have been able to find, is contained in a legal document which is preserved at Dunvegan. This is dated in 1527, and in it Lord Lovat values the 14 merklands he owned in Glenelg at £40 Scots a year, or £3 6s 8d sterling. The value of the merkland is 4s 8½d sterling.

The next piece of evidence is a rental of Kintire and Islay, which is printed in the appendix to Vol. 2 of "The Clan Donald," by Doctors MacDonald, of Killearnan and Kiltarlity. This I copy from that work :—

	North Kintyre.	South Kintire.	Islay.
Money	£125 10s 0d Scots	£162 8s 4d Scots.	£45 0s 1d Scots
Meal.............	388¾ stones	480 stones	2593 stones
Malt	4 chalders 10 bolls:	25 chalders 14 bolls	—
	= 74 bolls	= 414 bolls	
Marts	6	48	301
Cows	1	—	—
Muttons	41	53	301
Cheese	307¾ stones	342¼ stones	301 stones
Geese	—	—	301
Poultry	—	—	301

Total Money Value of the Three Estates.

Money	£322 18 6	£332 18 5
Meal—3061¾ stones at 2s, should be 3461¾	366 2 10	346 3 6
Malt—30 chalders 8 bolls at 5s the boll ...	122 2 6	122 0 0
Marts—356 at 2 merks	553 6 8	474 13 4
Mutton—595 at 2s, should be 395	45 11 10	39 10 0
Cheese—951½ stones at 5s a stone	237 2 0	237 17 6
Geese—301 at 4d	} 6 0 4	7 10 6
Poultry—301 at 2d		

Total in Scots money £1666 2 11 £1560 13 3

In the rental, which is copied in column 1, a great many mistakes in calculating the amounts and value of produce appear. These I have corrected in column 2.

The prices of produce in 1542 are worth noting. Meal was twopence a boll, a mart two shillings and twopence, a sheep was twopence ; you could have bought three geese or

six chickens for a penny.   The number of stones in a **boll**
varied in different counties, and even in different parts of **the**
same county. At Campbelltown, in Kintire, it was ten stones,
and I have made my calculations on that basis.

I do not know the number of merklands in Kintire. In
Islay there were 360. It is probable that the Chief kept **59**
in his own hands, and that the remaining 301 were in the **hands**
of the tenants. South Kintire was worth £273 14s 8d ; North
Kintire, £468 7s 8d ; Islay, £818 10s 11d. The total value
was £1560 13s 3d Scots, or £130 0s 11½d sterling. The value
of the merkland in Islay was £2 14s 5d Scots, or about 4s 6d
sterling. Considering how closely the new valuation and the
values in Glenelg and Islay agree, we may be fairly certain
that the value of the merkland in the early 16th century was
about 4s 6d.   A much lower percentage of the rent was paid
in money in Islay than in Kintire. The reason probably was
that the Chief's castle was in Islay, and that he wanted larger
supplies of food for the maintenance of his household.

At Dunvegan are two discharges, dated 1571, from Alexander Bayne of Tulloch for monies paid to him on account
of the " terce " owned by his wife as the widow of one of the
MacLeod Chiefs. These make it clear that a considerable rise
had taken place, and I think that the value of the merkland
was then about 9s.

Much information is given as to values in the report on
the Islands, written between 1577 and 1595 for the information of the King, but I am convinced that this report is
entirely without any value. A clause in it makes it clear
that the writer had never visited the Islands he pretended to
describe, and his account of them is amazingly inaccurate.
For instance, he says that " Skye is 40 miles long, and 40
broad, and almost round."   The figures, moreover, which he
gives cannot be correct. According to him the amount of
different kinds of produce paid as rent in Islay is from 14 to
56 times what it had been in 1542. We know from other
sources that the King held most exaggerated ideas concerning
the value of land in the Islands, and the rents he might exact
for them. Probably these notions were based on such reports
as this, which were very likely furnished to him by unscru-

pulous persons, who wished to give him information which would be pleasing to him. For these reasons I reject this report as valueless.

In 1610, the Dunvegan Chief bought 12 merklands in Waternish from Lord Kintail, paying 9000 merks for them, or £500 sterling. Land then changed hands at 20 years' purchase. Therefore, we may assume that the annual value was £25. If this is correct, the value of the merkland had risen to £2 1s 8d sterling.

This calculation is to some extent verified by the evidence of a tack, the terms of which were given in an earlier chapter. This tack is dated 1625. In it Clan Ranald lets 4½ merklands. Allowing for the grassum which was to be paid, I calculate the rent at 180 merks, or £10 0s 0d sterling. The value of the merkland is £2 4s 4d, a slight increase on the value I calculated for 1610. I think that these two values confirm each other.

The increased values in 1610 and 1625 show that even in the earlier year the West Highlands were beginning to settle down, and that the beneficent effects of the agreements reached at Iona in the preceding year were beginning to be felt.

In 1644 the first Valuation Roll was made for the Sheriffdom of Inverness, including Ross. Up to this date, except in the rental of 1542, we have had no definite figures to go on, and all our values have been obtained by inference and deduction, but in 1644 we are on firmer ground. This valuation shows that an amazing increase on the rents in 1625 had taken place. In that year the merkland had been worth £2 4s 4d. In 1644 it had risen to £9 12s 4d ; in other words, land was worth more than four times what had been its value twenty years earlier, and even this may be under the mark. We do not know whether any deductions on the gross rent were allowed, whether or not payments for cess and teinds were included, or whether any grassums had been paid, and the rent reduced in consequence. For these reasons the real value may have been materially higher ; it cannot well have been lower.

This valuation, and one made in 1691, will be found in " Antiquarian Notes," by Fraser-Mackintosh. From it I take the value of the estates held by the Western Chiefs in the Sheriffdom ; some also owned property in other countries. I have reduced Scots money to sterling.

MacLeod, upwards of	...	...	£15,000	=	£1250 0 0
Seaforth, upwards of	...	...	14,000	=	1166 13 4
Argyll, upwards of ...	...	...	13,000	=	1083 6 8
MacDonald of Sleat, upwards of	...	10,000	=	833 6 8	
Clanranald, upwards of	...	...	9000	=	750 0 0

Value of merkland, £115 8s 5d Scots or £9 12s 4d sterling.

The next piece of evidence which we possess is a rental of the MacLeod estate in Skye, which was compiled in 1664. The original is, unfortunately, lost, but a copy was printed by Mr MacDonald of Skeabost in a pamphlet which he published about forty years ago.

For the purposes of comparison I give the Islay rental of 1542 side by side with the Skye rental of 1664 :—

1542.

The money rent was 3s per each merkland	...	...	£45 0 1
Meal, 259⅓ bolls, at £1 0s 0d the boll	...	...	259 6 8
Each merkland paid 1 mart, i.e., 301 at £1 6s 8d...	...	401 6 8	
„ „ 1 mutton, i.e., 301 at 2s	...	...	30 2 0
„ „ 1 stone of cheese, 301 at 5s ...	...	75 5 0	
„ „ 1 goose, i.e., 301 at 4d	...	...	5 0 4
„ „ 1 head of poultry, i.e., 301 at 2d	...	2 10 2	

Scots money ...	...	...	...	...	£818 10 11
Sterling money	...	...	...	...	68 4 3

Value of merkland—£2 14s 5d Scots, 4s 6d sterling.

1664.

Money	...	...	...	...	...	...	...£8081 13 4
Cess ...	...	...	...	...	...	...	... 614 10 0
Teinds	...	...	...	...	...	...	... 1611 13 4
Mart money ...	...	...	...	...	...	... 415 0 0	
309¼ bolls, ½ beare ½ meal, at £5 6s 8d	...	...	...1614 0 0				
Hens at 3s a dozen ...	...	...	...	...	... 141 16 8		
399½ stones, ½ butter, ½ cheese, at £2 2s 0d...	...	... 814 13 4					
292 wedders at £1 6s 8d	...	...	...	...	... 389 6 8		
Horse corn at £3 0s 0d a boll	...	...	...	... 210 16 8			

Total in Scots money...	...	...	£13,961 3 1	
Total in sterling	...	...	...	... 1163 8 4

Value of merkland, £183 13s 11d Scots, £15 6s 2d sterling.

Islay contained 360 merklands ; 301 merklands were let, and dealt with in the rent roll. The Skye estate only contained 76 merklands, all of which were let. Allowing for this, we first notice the vast increase in the amount of the produce paid to the landowner. In 1542, 1 mutton or wedder, 1 stone of cheese, and less than a boll of meal were paid for each merkland ; in 1664, nearly 4 wedders, 5½ stones of cheese and butter, and 4 bolls of meal were paid for each merkland.

Prices also had greatly increased in 1664. Meal now was more than five times what it had been in 1542, wedders 13 times, cheese 5 times and marts 9 times.

These increases in the amount and the value of produce caused an enormous rise in the value of land. The total value of the Islay estate in 1664 was probably over £4600 a year, compared with £68 4s 3d in 1542.

The early rent rolls are documents of great interest. Some are called judicial rentals because they were made by the Baron Court, not because they were made by any outside body. The proceedings at the meetings of the Baron Court are fully described. The names of the tenants are given, and the extent of their farms is added in penny lands.

The rentals were ruled in columns, one for each head of payment. The first four require some explanation. Though a large percentage of the rent was nominally paid in money, probably none of it was really so paid. Every year a large drove of cattle, with possibly some other exports, was sent to market from the estate. Each tenant sent his stock to go south with the drove ; the factor credited him with the stock he sent, sold them at the market, retained what was due to the landlord, paying it over to the laird's " doer " in Edinburgh, and handed over the balance to the tenant.

Cess was the land tax due to the Government. I think from the amount of cess paid by the tenants that they paid half the cess to the landlord, leaving him to pay it over with his own half to the commissioners of supply for the county, who in their turn paid it over to the Government.

Teinds are the payments known as tithes in England. The tenants paid the whole of these. The Scottish law of

10

teinds is most complicated, and I shall only attempt to explain the appearance of a column for teinds on the credit side in these rent rolls.

Under an Act of Parliament, passed in 1590, the teinds had been fixed at 20 per cent. of the rent. Till a " decree of locality " was obtained, this 20 per cent. was payable, varying with the amount of the rent. It will be observed that in this rental the amount given for teinds is almost exactly 20 per cent. of the money rent. When a " decree of locality " was obtained, the rent at the date of this decree was taken as the basis, and the teinds were fixed at 20 per cent. of that amount for all time coming. On this estate the decree was obtained in 1753.

The teinds were divided into two parts. In the seventeenth century one-third of the teinds in the Diocese of the Isles, and one-fourth in the Diocese of Argyle, belonged to the bishop, but this third or fourth was charged with the maintenance of the churches, the building and upkeep of the manses, and with the provision of the elements used at the Holy Communion. This share of the teinds passed in 1690 to the Synod of Argyle, and ultimately to the Crown. The landowners generally held these teinds under tacks from the bishop, and later on from the Synod of Argyle and the Crown, paying a tack duty and fulfilling the obligations. The earliest tack of teinds at Dunvegan is dated in 1621. The tack duty was £2 10s 0d.

On this estate, the proprietor being " patron and titular " of the benefices on the property, the remaining two-thirds belonged to him ; but these teinds were charged with payments to the clergy, the amount of which was fixed from time to time by the Court of Session. This explains the reason why payments for teinds were included in the rental.

As has been explained in an earlier chapter, the marts were beasts which were killed in autumn, and salted down for use in winter. When a farm was not large enough to pay a mart, some "mart money " was payable. Of the payments in kind little need be said. In early days when the Chiefs maintained large establishments of retainers in their castles, they required enormous quantities of food. In the 1542 rental 95 per cent.

of the total rent was paid in kind. But as time went on smaller households were maintained, less food was wanted, and a larger proportion of the rent was nominally paid in money.

An old rental, exhaustive as it seems, does not necessarily give the full values of the land at the time. It was the custom that grassums, which were sums of money paid on the renewal of a lease, should be paid. Long as were the periods of time for which tacks were then granted, the grassums must have very materially decreased the rent of the farms. I have before me a tack of Strond, in Harris, in the year 1657. In this the grassum paid is 500 merks, the period is " all the days of his life and of his lawful sone's life, and 19 years after; " the rent was 80 merks money, 12 bolls victual, 16 stones half-cheese, half-butter, 6 custom wedders, and one custom mart. This lease for two lives and nineteen years had fallen in by 1698, for I find Strond rented in that year at 140 merks.

Grassums were very often exacted. One was payable under Clanranald's tack in 1625, and over £4000 was paid in grassums in 1754.

There is yet another reason for doubting whether a rent roll gives the full value of the estate at the time. It was the custom to give charters for life of land to the widow of a deceased Chief in payment of her jointure, and to his younger children in payment of their portions, and this land in life-rent was not included in the rental. In 1644, out of the £15,000 Scots which the MacLeod estate was then worth, over £4000 was in life-rent, and this would not have been included in a rent-roll.

Towards the end of the seventeenth century there was a drop both in prices and in rents, but about 1740 both began to rise. In 1754 the rental of the MacLeod estate was close on £3000, in 1769 it was over £4000. After this large parts of the estate were sold, and I can only estimate values on the whole estate. During the closing years of the 18th century both prices and rents were rising very fast. I estimate the rental about 1800 at about £7000. In 1811, for reasons which I have explained in an earlier chapter, it leapt up to £21,000 ; in 1825 it dropped to £15,000. In 1860 it had risen to £18,000 ; in 1881, when rents had reached their zenith, it was nearly £26,000, and the value of the merkland was £192 14s 6d.

When we remember that in early days the value of the merkland was 1s 1⅓d, and that the value of the estate had been £6 15s 0d a year, it is indeed an amazing rise.

The reasons for this rise are manifold. The increase which took place between 1610 and 1664 is accounted for by the fact that in the interval clan feuds had ceased, trade had revived, and the tackmen, having been released from rendering onerous services, were able to pay a higher rent.

The increase which took place between the beginning of the 18th century and the end of the 19th was mainly caused by the remarkable increase in prices which then occurred. After carefully going through a great number of old bills and accounts, I have arrived at the conclusion that, in 1701, the purchasing power of money was 12½ times as great as it was in 1881 ; about 1750 7 times as great ; about 1770 5½ times. If we multiply the rental of the MacLeod estate at three times by the factors named, we shall get a fairly constant result, about 20 per cent. less than the value in 1881.

1701 ...... £1603 × 12½	...	... =	£20,038
1754 ...... £2994 × 7	...	... =	£20,958
1777 ...... £3757 × 5½	...	... =	£20,658

1881—Actual value—£25,706. Most of this is now in other hands.

I conclude therefore that about 80 per cent. of the increase was caused by the rise in prices.

Other reasons contributed to cause the increase. Up to 1811 the farms, houses and buildings belonged to the tenants. Now the landlord has to provide them and keep them in repair. A farm, with a house and farm buildings, naturally commands a higher rent than one which has none. Much draining and fencing have been done, roads have been made, steamers have begun to ply, communications have greatly improved, and shooting tenants pay high rents, which naturally swell the gross value of a property, though they may not greatly increase its net value. These account for the 20 per cent. of the increase which was not caused by the rise in prices.

In England also there has been a remarkable rise in the value of land. I know of one estate in Northumberland which was sold for £100 about 1520, the gross rental of which is now about £1800 a year. I give some particulars concerning another estate in the same county which show the same thing.

Two *inquisitiones post mortem* relating to the owners of the Manor of Ulgham give interesting information as to the value of land in Northumberland in 1436 and 1517. The manor extends to 2675 acres. In 1436 only 380 acres, in 1517 1070 acres were cultivated, the rest was waste land. The rental in 1436 was £8 3s 4d, in 1517 £18 13s 4d. In 1436 arable land was rented at 6 pence an acre, in 1517 at 1s an acre. In 1436 pasture land was rented at $2\frac{2}{5}$d per acre, in 1517 at 1s 3d an acre. Cottages at both periods were rented at 2s a year.

Common land, not mentioned in 1436, was valued in 1517 at $\frac{1}{4}$d per 20 acres. The rental in 1861 was £2662, an increase of 334 times from 1436, and an increase of 121 times from 1517. Ulgham Grange, extending to 703 acres, belonged to Newminster Abbey. In 1541 its value was £13 6s 8d ; in 1861 £807, an increase of 60 times. The smaller increase in the value of a monastic estate emphasises the fact that the monks cultivated their estates better than the lay owners of land did.

THE BURDENS ON LAND.

In the old days of the Norse occupation these were nil. Later on they were limited to the payments which had to be made to the superior Lord under the feudal system, the maintenance of the ships for the King's service, the payment of a fine on succession (the germ of the death duties), of another on marriage, and the rights of wardship during a minority. These last meant that, after the maintenance and education of the heir were provided for, all the profits of the estate went to the superior Lord. These were called the nomentries, and were often sold by the King, as those of the Dunvegan estate were in 1585. In a charter dated 1611 they were commuted for an annual payment of £8 10s 0d, and the fine on marriage fixed at £25.

Later on other taxation was imposed, though these former claims continued.

I shall deal with the outgoings under five heads : 1, Cess ; 2, Payments to Ministers ; 3, Schools ; 4, Charity ; 5, Management. N.B.—All the payments which follow are given in sterling money.

1. *The Cess, or Land Tax.* This, I think, was imposed early in the seventeenth century. The earliest receipt at Dunvegan for cess is dated 1617. Cess was payable quarterly, at Candlemas in February, Whitsuntide in May, at Lammas in August, and at Martinmas in November ; but only 2½ months' cess was exacted each quarter : probably a rough method of allowing deductions on the gross value. Interest was payable on overdue cess. Failure to pay led to a troop of horse being quartered on the delinquent till he paid up.

I cannot give the amount of the charges until 1640. In that year it was 18 per cent. of the assessed value. Between 1660 and 1690 it averaged about 21 per cent. In that year the cess was fixed on a permanent footing. The then value of the land was taken as the basis of assessment, and no change has been made since, although the value of the land has much increased.

The idea was that cess should be levied at the rate of four shillings in the pound, but I find that the actual payments were generally considerably less. Possibly the old custom of only calling for 2½ months' cess each quarter may have continued, but I have also found a note that in some years the commissioners of supply for the county, who managed the business, did not find it necessary to call for more than eight months' cess, or in some years for more than six months' cess. I do not understand the reason for this.

Very occasionally they found it necessary to make increased demands on the taxpayers. In 1779 an extra 6 per cent. was called for.

Besides this regular taxation, Parliament occasionally made grants to the King for special purposes. In 1617 such a grant was made for " the reparation of His Majesties buildings in Scotland "; in 1648 for the maintenance of " a garisone at Inverlochy "; in 1679 2½ months' cess was granted " to make up the defect of the Excyse." Several times payments were demanded for the repair of bridges in different parts of Scotland which had been swept away by floods.

2. *Payments of the Clergy.* As we have seen, a landowner, who was " patron and titular " of the benefices on his estate, and held a tack from the bishop of the latter's share of the teinds, owned all the teinds, but out of them he had heavy payments to make. He had to keep the churches in repair, to provide and keep in repair the manses, to supply the elements for the Holy Communion, and to make such payments as were ordered by the Court of Session to the ministers.

In the seventeenth and early eighteenth centuries the ministers received £50 a year each. Besides this they received some meal and wedders, which were probably teinds on the rent paid in kind ; and in addition each of them, then as now, had a glebe. In Harris the minister received £8 6s 8d in lieu of a manse and glebe. Thus the clergy were better paid then than now. Assuming that, in 1750, the purchasing power of money was seven times what it now is, a minister was receiving the equivalent of £350 a year, instead of the much smaller sums most Highland ministers now receive. At that time probably a landowner was making some profit out of the teinds. I estimate his total outgoings under this head at 12½ per cent. to 15 per cent. of the gross rentals, and the teinds he received were 20 per cent.; but, as time went on, the Court of Session raised the amount of stipend payable to ministers, till all the teinds were absorbed. Then all the landowner's profit from the teinds came to an end. But if he had obtained a " decree of locality " the teinds, instead of rising, as they would otherwise have done, with the increased rent, remained a fixed sum, which was an ever-decreasing percentage of the rentals.

On some estates, where such a decree was not obtained, the burden of teinds has been a very heavy one indeed, especially in recent years. But landlords who obtained a decree of locality cannot be blamed because the arrangement then made has turned out favourably to them. Had rents fallen instead of rising, it would have been a bad arrangement for them, and in the 17th and 18th centuries no one foresaw the amazing rise which has actually taken place.

3. *Payments to Schoolmasters.* From the beginning of the 18th century there were schools on each of the estates. They cost the landlords about £5 sterling each. Later on each cost about £11.

In addition to these sums, found by the estate, there was a subscription for this purpose by the tenants ; it must not be assumed that these sums were the whole salary teachers received.

4. *Charity.* In those days there were no poor rates. The people were extremely independent, and took a pride in maintaining their own poor relations ; but there were always a few in receipt of " pensions " from the proprietor. These payments, though nominally voluntary, were really compulsory, and must be looked on as charges on the estate. Schoolmasters and charity together did not cost more than 2 per cent. of the rental.

5. *Management.* On each estate there was a factor, though sometimes the Skye and Harris factorships were combined. The Harris factor was called the " Chalmerlayne," and received a salary of £12 10s. The Skye factor received £33 6s 8d. The Glenelg factor received £27 15s 6d. They collected the rents, arranged for the sale of rents in kind, made all the local payments, rendered their accounts of charge and discharge, and paid over the balance either to the proprietor himself or his Edinburgh " doer."

In the 18th century the factor was generally one of the gentlemen tacksmen on the estate. I give a summary of an old paper in which his duties are defined.

He should frequently visit the farms, and observe the methods followed by the tenants, correcting their errors, and encouraging their improvements. No sub-letting of land is to be allowed to sons or sons-in-law. No more horses shall be kept than the cultivation of the land requires. Dykes must be built of stone, and not of turf. Peats may only be cut in places indicated by the ground officer. Soil is not to be doubled over on the riggs. The keeping of goats is forbidden on account of the harm they do to trees. The factor is to deal with disputes about marches, and is to take steps to prevent poaching : the gentlemen tacksmen can get leave to shoot.

Under the factor were ground officers, one in each district. Up to 1750 their salaries were £2 4s 5d a year. In that year they were raised to £3 3s 4d.

Besides these local officials was a man of business in Edinburgh, called a " doer," who received a regular salary, and managed all the affairs of the Chief. Before 1697 the doer's salary was only about £13 a year. In that year it was raised to £50, at which it remained through the 18th century.

I calculate outgoings under the head of management at about 7 per cent., growing rather less as rents rose.

Highland landlords in early days knew nothing of the charges which affect their successors so grievously. Up to the beginning of the 19th century the farmhouses were the property of the tenants ; and the only repairs the proprietor had to pay for were those on his own house, the manses, and the mills, which had been built about 1730, and were sources of revenue to the estate. County assessments for " rogue money," the quaint term applied to money spent on the administration of justice, and " contingencies," which mainly meant the salaries of county officials, do not appear till early in the 19th century.

Payments for roads first appear in the late 18th century. Poor rates were not imposed till 1845, education rates till 1872.

On the other hand, rents being still low, the fixed charges of cess and teinds were much heavier burdens on an early proprietor than on his successors. Late in the 18th century, and early in the 19th century, there was a short period during which, rents having risen, and the fresh charges not having been yet imposed, the percentage required for out-goings was very low ; but, since then, it has been steadily rising, and has now reached a level which in many cases leaves no margin at all.

I have not been able to estimate outgoings before 1645.
The following table gives the percentages of the gross rent,
which were absorbed by outgoings at the times named :—

1645—1660 about	38 per cent.		
1660—1690 ,,	35	,,	
1690—1754 ,,	35	,, gradually falling to about
1754—1769 ,,	18¾	,, 30 per cent. Great rises
1769—1811 ,,	14	,, in rent took place in
1811—1825 ,,	6	,, 1754, 1769, and 1811.

In this table I have only included the outgoings mentioned
above. Early in the 19th century new burdens, such as
county assessments and " meliorations," began to be felt.
This last is the word employed to describe expenses incurred
for the building and repair of farm houses and steadings. For
this reason the outgoings during the later years mentioned in
the table were undoubtedly heavier than the percentages
given. If we include expenditure on roads, fencing, draining,
and other improvements, they were very much heavier.

Since 1825 poor rates, education and highway rates have
been imposed, and in Scotland the landlords pay half the
rates. Buildings have become a heavy drain, and probably
now a Highland proprietor's outgoings amount to something
like 70 or 80 per cent. of his gross rent, and on the balance he
has to pay income tax. But these and the many other events
affecting the land which have taken place during the last
hundred years are outside the scope of this chapter.

The ownership of the foreshores is a question which
vitally affects all the owners of Scotch estates which lie on the
sea. The foreshores comprise the land which lies between
the high and low water-marks ; their owner has several valuable privileges. He can build a pier on them, and collect dues
from the ships which use that pier ; he can cut the sea-ware
that grows on the foreshores ; he can erect a weir for the
purpose of catching fish ; he is entitled to any wreckage which
may be cast up on the shore.

In England the foreshores belong to the Crown, and the
authorities in Scotland are always claiming them in that
country also.

There is no doubt that the foreshores belong to the owner of the adjoining soil when they are specially granted in the charters under which the land is held, or when the owner's estate forms part of what was a free barony ; but it is a moot point whether, under Scottish law, they belong to proprietors who cannot claim them on one or other of these grounds.

CHAPTER X.

SOME ISLAND FOLK-LORE.

I should imagine that no country in the world is richer in folk-lore than the West Highlands. The ceilidh was an institution, and our people loved to gather together on a winter's evening, and to tell each other again and again the old stories which they had received from their forbears.

Many of these traditions are of great historical interest. They record, more or less accurately, events which really happened in the past, and, indeed, the history of every clan largely depends on information obtained from this source. Many of the old stories which relate to my own clan have been recorded in my two volumes on the History of the MacLeods. One or two of those which follow I have heard since these books were written, and two or three more, which are specially interesting because they throw so much light on the super-stition of our forefathers, I have ventured to repeat. I am under the impression that some of them have never been published.

Some of the traditions were given to me by the late Miss Emily MacLeod, some by my venerable friend, Miss Tolmie, and a great many by Mr John Mackenzie, the factor at Dun-vegan, all three of whom got them from old people who had often heard them told at ceilidhs.

These old stories are worthy of careful study, for they reveal to us the character of the people who loved to tell them, and enable us to form an idea concerning their beliefs, their ideals, and their fancies.

There are two methods of telling these traditions. The first is the one adopted by J. F. Campbell, in his " Popular Tales of the West Highlands." In this he gives a literal translation of the Gaelic in which he heard them. A single short story told in this manner has a charm of its own, but, when many stories are told, I think that this method becomes tiresome and monotonous. I have, therefore, arrived at the conclusion that it is better to tell the stories in my own words, only occasionally preserving a quaint bit of phraseology. The first two tales in my collection are love stories. They show how highly our fathers valued the great qualities of constancy and fidelity.

A TALE OF TRUE LOVE.

There was great joy at Dunvegan. The bridal morning of the Chief's daughter had arrived. The cooks in the great kitchen of the castle were busy preparing the bridal banquet, troops of glad clansmen came singing along, the sound of the pipes filled the air, the bards were serenading the maiden, she herself was being attired for the occasion with joy in her heart, for she dearly loved the young, fair-haired Chief, who was coming from Lewis to claim his fair bride, and to stand at the altar with her at his side.

The bridegroom might arrive at any minute. Even now they knew that his galley was speeding across the Minch to bring him to his bride. But, fine as the early morning had been, there suddenly sprang up a tremendous gale of wind, one of those appalling storms which we West Highlanders know so well. The sounds of rejoicing were hushed, fear gripped every heart. Could any boat live in such a sea ? was the sad question which men asked of each other. Time passed, the bridegroom did not come. The maiden kept hoping against hope that his galley would weather the storm. but at last a sickening fear turned to a dreadful certainty, They knew that they would never see him again ; for he must have been lost in the Minch, with the whole of his train.

The maiden was heart-broken. As the leaden-footed days passed by, she slowly pined away, and at length the last day of her life dawned. She knew that she was dying, and she made one last request before she passed away. She besought her father that she might be buried in the sea, so that she might lie beside her true love till the crack of doom. Her father gave her his promise, and soon after she died.

The Chief had promised, but could he fulfil his word ?
It seemed a dreadful thing to cast his daughter's body into the
cold, cruel sea. It seemed a shocking thing that no memorial
stone should stand over her grave, to tell future generations
how a maiden of their race had died for love. He felt that
he could not do it, and in spite of the promise which he had
given, he resolved to take her remains to Rodel, and lay
her in the sacred earth where already reposed so many scions
of his ancient line.

The galley put to sea, and started on its sad voyage
across the Minch in fine weather. But before they had got
beyond Dunvegan Head, again a fierce and sudden gale sprang
up. They could not go on ; they must put back. But, the
Chief asked himself, was this gale a mere chance ? Was it not
a message from heaven, which bade him fulfil the solemn promise which he had made to his daughter ? He decided that
this was what the gale meant.

He reverently took the shrunken form of his daughter
in his arms, and, his heart filled with sorrow, cast her on the
waves.

Then there was seen a strange and wondrous sight. A
grand majestic form, the figure of him the maid had loved so
well, rose from the sea. He clasped his love in his arms, and
those two, whose fair young lives had been blighted on earth,
sank together beneath the waves, there in the ocean's caves
to lie till the sea shall give up her dead, and death be finally
conquered.

Nature herself preserves the memory of this strange
bridal. However wild the seas which break upon our Northern shores, there is ever one spot where perfect calm for ever
reigns. That is the place where these faithful lovers, separ-
ated by death, were in death re-united.

In 1566, Torquil Oighre, the heir of the Lewis branch of
the MacLeods, was drowned, with his train of sixty men,
when crossing over from Lewis to Skye. It is quite likely that
he was on his way to Dunvegan to claim his bride, and that
this story has some foundation in fact. In that case the
maiden must have been a daughter of Tormod, the 11th of
the Dunvegan Chiefs.

MARY OF MARRIG.

Mary, the daughter of the farmer at Marrig, in Harris, was a very lovely girl, and being, moreover, an heiress in a small way, she had a great many suitors. Among them was their neighbour, the tenant of Hushinish. He had won her father's good-will, but as he could not obtain Mary's, his wooing was no more prosperous than that of the other aspirants to her hand.

In course of time a new candidate for Mary's favour appeared on the scene, who succeeded in winning her affection, and who himself became devotedly attached to her. This was Archibald, a younger son of the Earl of Argyll. This young man had killed one of the Frasers of Aird in a duel, and had sought refuge in Harris from the revenge of his adversary's kindred. This proved to be a fatal bar to the success of his suit. When Mary's father heard that he had killed a Fraser, to which clan his loved wife had belonged, he absolutely refused to sanction the match, and insisted that Campbell should leave Harris, and never see his daughter again. Before Archibald left he had a farewell interview with his lady love. He declared that he would wait for any length of time, if only he could make her his wife in the end, and she, giving him a knot of blue ribbon as a token of constancy, vowed that she would marry no other man while he lived. He then went away, and took up a seafaring life.

For some years nothing was heard of him, but Mary remained faithful, and refused to listen to any other suitor. At last a vessel put into Marrig Bay. On board of this ship were three sailors, who said that they had known and loved Archibald, and that he had been drowned some time before, to their great sorrow. When this became known, the farmer of Hushinish again began to press his suit. Mary's father used all his influence to induce her to accept him, and at last, though she could not forget Archibald, she agreed to marry Hushinish, and a day was fixed for the wedding.

Mary's father found that his cellar was insufficiently supplied with wine for the bridal feast, and he sailed away to

Loch Seaforth, hoping to find a vessel there, from the captain
of which he could purchase some wine. In the harbour of
Loch Seaforth a Dutch trader, laden with wine, was lying at
anchor. A bargain was soon struck, and the captain and mate
made themselves so agreeable that Marrig asked them to
come back with him and be present at the wedding. They
arrived just before the ceremony was to begin. The mate
went up to the bride and handed her a small parcel, saying in
a low tone, " As a token of my undying devotion." The parcel
contained her own knot of blue ribbon. She looked up, and,
recognising him, flung herself into his arms, crying, " My own
beloved Archie."

The consternation of the wedding party was great. The
bridegroom, realising that he had no chance, went away
home, bitterly disappointed, and old Marrig, touched by the
constancy and devotion of the lovers, withdrew his opposition
to their union. " The feast is ready," he said, " the minister
is here, we may have a wedding after all." So Archibald
stepped into the bridegroom's place, the ceremony which
made him and Mary one was performed, and the feast which
followed was the merriest ever known in Harris.

It is said that all the Campbells in Harris are descended
from Archibald Campbell and Mary of Marrig.

A HIGHLAND WILLIAM TELL.

A man, named Fearchar Dubh, who seems to have been
a very lawless sort of person, killed a sheep belonging to a
neighbour, and when the owner of the sheep objected, killed
him too. He then fled in his boat, intending to go to Harris,
but a gale sprang up, and he was forced to land on an island
near Vaternish. Here MacLeod, who had been told of the
crime, and was pursuing Fearchar in his galley, found him.
Fearchar let off an arrow, which passed through MacLeod's
leg, and pinned him to the mast, saying as he did so, " I could
as easily have shot you through the body as through the
leg. I have spared your life ; I beseech you, let me escape."

Rightly or wrongly, the Chief agreed, and Fearchar went
to Harris. Here he lived for some years, but wearying of

exile from Skye, he returned, and going to Dunvegan, implored the Chief to pardon him.

MacLeod agreed on a condition. He sent for Fearchar's brother, and ordered his men to place an egg on the brother's head. Then, addressing Fearchar, he said—" You are a famous shot with the bow ; if your arrow strikes the egg off your brother's head, you will be pardoned ; if you fail to do so, you will die." Fearchar shot his arrow, and struck the egg, so winning his pardon, but he said to MacLeod—" I have two arrows ; had I missed the egg and killed my brother, the second one was for you."

The reader will notice the resemblance of this story to that of William Tell.

In the old days there was living in every district a " wise man," possibly one or two wise men, to whom the people were wont to refer their difficulties and disputes. I imagine that they had no learning, but they were remarkably shrewd, and some of them, I fancy, practised, or pretended to practice, the black arts. One of the most famous of these was Aodh or Hugh MacQueen, who lived in the latter part of the 17th century It was he, whose decision in a difficult case, is related in the following story :—

A cow, belonging to a man named Donald, fell over a cliff into a boat, which happened to be lying below the rock, and which was the property of a man named Tormod. The cow was killed, and the boat was damaged. Tormod claimed the cost of repairing the boat on the ground that it had been injured by Donald's cow ; the latter claimed the value of the cow on the ground that, if the boat had not been where it was, his cow would have fallen into deep water, and have escaped with its life.

MacLeod, to whom the matter was referred, found some difficulty in coming to a decision, and accompanied the men to a " wise " man who lived near. This was rather a famous person, named Aodh (or Hugh) MacQueen. The sage only

11

asked one question, "Who was the owner of the rock from which the cow had fallen?" He was told that MacLeod owned the rock. "Then," said the sage, "MacLeod must pay for both the cow and the boat; for if MacLeod's rock had not been there the cow would not have fallen over it, and the boat would not have been injured." MacLeod good-naturedly assented, and so the dispute was settled.

Quite often tales were told at the Ceilidhs about the old Ossianic heroes. One of these will be found in the story about the fairies' house on Hallaval Mor. Another follows :—

A LEGEND OF LOCH DUNVEGAN.

At one time Fionn, the famous Ossianic hero, was living, with his six sons, on an island in Loch Dunvegan. One day they saw a tall woman, with one eye in the middle of her forehead, walking on the sea towards them. She attacked them, and they had great difficulty in keeping her at bay. At last Diarmid, Fionn's eldest son, said—"I will keep her occupied while you dig a hole, and, when it is finished, we can put her into it." So they dug the hole, the woman was thrown in, and, I suppose, buried alive.

The next day they saw the fairy blacksmith coming over the hill, accompanied by his black cat. He was very tall, and, though he had only one leg, covered ten yards of ground at each hop. He asked if they had seen the woman with one eye, and when he heard what they had done with her, told them that they could only kill her if they put her at the bottom of the sea. He then went away, travelling so fast that they found it difficult as they followed to keep him in sight; but Diarmid, who was the swiftest runner of them all, succeeded in doing so, and saw him enter the fairy smithy.

Diarmid followed him, and found several fairy smiths, each with four hands, at work making a sword, singing a song as they did so, just as the makers of Siegfrid's sword did. "There is only one way to temper the sword," said the fairy blacksmith, "and that is to run it through the first person who enters the smithy." Diarmid was much afraid that one of his brothers, who he knew must be at hand, might come in;

but as it happened, the fairy blacksmith's own mother was the
person who appeared at the door. Her son, without any
compunction, ran her through, and thus the sword was
tempered. He gave it to Diarmid, and he passed it on to his
father, who thus became possessed of his magic sword, with
which he could reach out three yards every way.

This and one or two of the other stories which are related
in this chapter also appear in Mr Seton Gordon's book, " The
Charm of Skye."

Perhaps our fathers delighted in tales of the supernatural more than in any others. Innumerable tales are told
about persons who possessed the second sight.

The following story is related by Martin, who says that
Sir Norman MacLeod, of Bernera, with whom he was well
acquainted, vouched for its truth.

A gentleman, who lived in Harris, was constantly being
seen by men who had the gift of the second sight with an
arrow in his thigh. They expected that he would be wounded
in his thigh in some fray ; but he died without anything
happening to him. It chanced on the day when his body
was brought to St Clement's at Rodel for burial, not in a
coffin, but lying on a bier, that the remains of another gentleman reached the church-yard at the same time. A quarrel
arose between the two parties as to which funeral should take
place first ; a fight ensued, and some arrows were let loose.
Sir Norman succeeded in quelling the disturbance ; but when
it was ended, it was found that an arrow had pierced the thigh
of the dead man as he lay on his bier.

It is an extraordinary fact that the predictions of men
and women who possessed the second sight so often were
fulfilled.

But sometimes a seer drew a mistaken inference from
what he had seen. One of these men once saw in a boat a
corpse, and a number of men whom he recognised as Mac-
Leod's relations. From this he inferred that MacLeod was
going to die. MacLeod did not die, but MacLean of Torloisk
did. MacLeod, with a number of his relations, happened to
be in Mull when Torloisk died. MacLeod and his relations

attended the funeral, the former going by land, the latter going by sea with the corpse in a boat. What the seer had seen happened, but he had drawn the wrong conclusion from it.

Another belief which was universally accepted amongst the Highlanders in the old days was that certain gifted mortals amongst them possessed the power of foretelling the future. The most famous of these prophets was Coinneach Odhar, or Kenneth Ouir, the Brahan Seer, who lived on the Mainland in the 17th Century. But a namesake of his, another Coinneach Odhar, who was born at Ness, in Lewis, at some period in the first quarter of the 16th Century, and lived in the island during the whole of his life, was no less remarkably gifted. Some writers have maintained that the two Coinneach Odhars were one and the same person, but, as one of them lived on the mainland in the 17th Century, and was burnt as a sorcerer, while the other lived in Lewis in the 16th Century, and was drowned, I do not see how this theory can be maintained. I have taken the following story of the Island seer from the Bannatyne MS. History of the MacLeods.

In my History of the MacLeods I have related the remarkable fulfilment of Kenneth's prophecy about the waving of the fairy flag for the third time at Dunvegan, and I need not repeat it here ; but the story which relates how Kenneth got his remarkable powers is so interesting that I think it will bear repetition.

The following is the correct version of how he obtained his supernatural powers :—

There was and still is an idea among Highlanders that the grave of a stranger ought to be purchased, otherwise the soul has no rest, and assumes its original corporeal appearance in its wanderings.

It being the duty of Kenneth's mother, on a particular night some time before he was born, to watch the corn-fields, as was always done in harvest, to prevent cattle from getting into the unenclosed fields, she sat down on an eminence overlooking a burial ground, and, having a rake and spindle with her, commenced her usual occupation of spinning. To her terror she saw a grave open, and the figure of a female in a strange garb issue from it. The figure proceeded to the sea, here close by, stretched her hands towards the ocean, and by her gestures seemed to express grief and woe.

Kenneth's mother, who was possessed of good nerves, soon recovered her presence of mind, and instantly resolved to become better acquainted with the unfortunate apparition. She signed herself with the sign of the Cross, and spoke the religious words most familiar to her. She hastened to the grave, laid her distaff across it, and sat down close by to await the return of its restless occupant.

The figure soon returned, and, finding it impossible to pass the earthly staff which was laid across the grave, addressed the mortal in most pathetic terms, and asked to be allowed to enter the grave. The other replied that she must first learn by what power she was enabled to leave it. The answer to this was as follows :—" I am a princess of a far-off and foreign land. I was lost at sea, and my body was thrown up upon this shore. It was found and deposited in this grave by the people of the country. As the earth has never been ransomed, my spirit cannot rest, and I am nightly obliged to wander down to the seashore and visit the spot where my body first touched the land. If you will purchase the earth in which my bones rest great will be your reward, and your name will descend to after ages as the mother of the most wonderful man of his time ; a handful of corn from one of your own fields will suffice."

The woman immediately cut a sheaf of corn and laid it in the grave. Before the apparition descended into her grave she put a small black and beautiful pebble into the woman's hand, saying—" Give this to the child which will be born to you when he is exactly seven years of age." She then went into the grave, which closed, and showed no appearance of having been opened. The woman kept the matter a secret, and shortly after became the mother of a boy, who was named Kenneth.

Years passed, and nothing out of the common occurred. On Kenneth's seventh birthday his mother, who had forgotten about her ghostly friend's admonition, wished the boy to go and call his father, who was at work in the fields some distance away, to his mid-day meal.   Kenneth was unwilling to go, till his mother, remembering the pebble, gave it him as the reward of his compliance with her wishes.

He took it in his hand, looked at it, and said—" A large whale is ashore in the Raven's Cave."   This was the first instance he gave of possessing supernatural powers, for it turned out that what he said was the case, and that a whale was actually ashore at the place he named, and from thenceforward his fame spread far and wide.

When he was about 50 years of age he prophecied the downfall and utter ruin of the MacLeods of Lewis.   This so enraged some of that Chief's followers that they waylaid him on a moor near the lake of Cangenvale, with a view to depriving him of the pebble, without which he could not prophecy.   He at once flung himself, still grasping the pebble, into the loch, preferring to lose his life rather than see his precious talisman fall into the hands of strangers.

Fairies were intensely real beings to the West Highlanders in old days.   I summarise their ideas about them.

Vast number of fairies inhabited the country.   They were " wee, wee people," I imagine about two feet high.   They lived in fairy mounds or hillocks.   Those who had the sight would see these mounds open, and the fairies come out.   They also had their homes in the old duns and brochs, which are so nummerous in our country, and could be heard by persons passing by, busily engaged on the churning of butter and weaving of cloth inside.

Fairies were very fond of wandering, and used to haunt the houses of human beings, sometimes considerably outstaying their welcome ; but they were very attached to their homes, and people, who wanted to get rid of them, found it was a good plan to get some one to come in and say, " The dun is on fire."   On hearing this the fairies would rush off to try and save their dwellings from destruction.

On the whole, the fairies were well disposed to their human friends, and often did them deeds of kindness.   A housewife would get up in the morning, and find that they had done all her housework for her during the night.   The reader will remember that a similar idea as to the good offices of fairies occurs in " The Merry Wives of Windsor."

But the fairies were extremely capricious, and ready to take offence. When they did take anything amiss, they would punish the offenders with great severity, sometimes keeping them prisoners in their fairy mounds for years.

They often stole cattle to furnish food for their banquets, leaving the skins of the stolen animals on the ground. Some of the fairies were wicked, malicious creatures, and would steal a mother's only child without pity or remorse.

In spite of these unpleasant traits in their characters, they were always spoken of as " the gude people." No one could tell that a fairy was not listening to what they said, and a few disrespectful words concerning them might be severely punished.

THE FAIRIES' HOUSE ON HALLAVAL MOR.

In the old days the fairies possessed an enormous underground house near the summit of Hallaval Mor, the larger of the two hills known as the MacLeod's Tables in Skye. Here once came Fionn or Fingal, the famous hero of Ossian, seeking winter quarters for the 900 men who accompanied him. The fairies extended their hospitality to him, and, so large was the house, his men were easily accommodated on one side of it. Soon after, one by one, the Kings of Greece and Spain, and another unnamed King arrived, each of them with 900 men, and room was found for the 2700 men on the other side of the house.

At Fionn's request the fairies brought in a bullock roasted whole for his men. The other men in the house wanted their share, and tried to pull away the tables on which the food was placed, but Fionn said that the whole bullock was not more than enough for his followers, and ordered them to hold the tables with one hand, while they ate with the other. Before long the 2700 men attacked Fionn, and he, with his 900 men, had to fight for their dinner. They completely defeated their assailants, and it is said that Fionn's dogs, Bran and Jaroch, killed even more men than he did with his magic sword. The fairies' house continued to exist through the ages, and fairies were often met on the hill. One day a man from Osdale met a very beautiful fairy, about three feet high, and some love passages passed between them. He, however, left her, and married the daughter of a neighbour.

In course of time his wife was expecting to become a mother, but was very far from well, so her husband, remembering his fairy friend, went off to ask her advice. Fearing that she might be jealous if she knew he had married another, he told her that it was his cow that was about to calve, and that it was ailing.

The fairy told him to rub his hand over the cow, and that that would be an effectual cure. She also gave him a bag of gold. This was so heavy that he could not even lift it, but the fairy said, " I will carry it for you," picked it up with the greatest ease, and carried it to his house. He rubbed his hand over his wife, she was completely cured, and soon after bore him a son.

The fairy found out the truth about his marriage, and, meeting him on the hill one day, told him that, to punish him for his deceit, she would take his son away from him. That very night the boy disappeared.

Ten years afterwards the man again met the fairy. She offered to let him see his son, and took him up to the house. Here he found his son, alive and well, and the fairy's parents, each of whom was a thousand years old. She told him that in another ten years she meant to marry his son, and gave him another bag of gold, once more carrying it home for him.

At the end of the ten years the man received an invitation to be present at the marriage of the fairy with his son. In the house he found a great assemblage of handsome men and beautiful women, and, though the narrator does not describe it, we may assume that the wedding took place. When her guest was leaving, the fairy gave him two bags of gold, carrying them home for him as before, and after that he saw her no more.

LURRAN AND THE FAIRIES.

Two brothers, who were on very bad terms, were joint tenants of the farm of Luskintire, in Harris. One of these was the foster son of a witch, who lived in a cottage on the farm. She had a son named Lurran, who possessed some of his mother's magical power, and could see things which were not revealed to the sight of ordinary mortals. He was also the swiftest runner in the country.

As the cornfields were not fenced, it was necessary that the cattle should be watched night and day, to prevent them from doing injury to the crops. One night Lurran, with some other young men, was employed on this work.

None of the others could see what he saw. A fairy mound opened, the fairies came out, and danced for a time on the green grass. They then came to the herd. The witch had put a charm on her foster son's cattle, and the fairies could not hurt them; but they selected two beasts belonging to the other brother, killed them, skinned them, and, leaving the skins full of offal on the ground, held a great feast in the fairy mound.

This happened again and again. Almost every morning the skins of two beasts were found, and they were always the animals belonging to one brother which were taken. Lurran, who alone could have explained the mystery, held his tongue, but the farmer who had lost so heavily was firmly persuaded that it was his brother who had done the mischief, and, brooding over his injuries, resolved to revenge himself when an opportunity came.

One night Lurran did a bold thing. He followed the fairies into the hill, and, sitting close to the entrance, partook of the fairies' banquet. When the feast was over, a cup filled with wine was passed round. When the cup came to Lurran, he seized it, spilt the contents, knowing that it was death to a mortal to drink the fairies' wine, and fled for his life. The infuriated fairies pursued him, but his swiftness of foot stood him in good stead, and he gained a stream which flowed down the hill near the fairy mound. Having crossed this, for the moment he was safe, for no fairy can cross running water. He made his way to his mother's cottage. She cast potent spells over the house, and this made it impossible for the fairies to enter. For some time Lurran never ventured to go out unless his mother had put a protecting spell on him, but one day he forgot, and went out with no charm on him. The fairies found him and killed him, and so avenged the theft of the cup.

A FAIRY TALE OF RHUANDHUNAN.

One hot summer day two women chanced to be walking by the Dun on the promontory at Rhuandhunan. They heard the fairies busily at work churning butter inside the Dun. One of the women, who was very hot and thirsty, said to her companion, "How I should like a glass of the buttermilk they have in there!"

The words were scarcely out of her mouth, when a wee, wee woman appeared, carrying a jug of buttermilk in her hands. She smiled pleasantly on the thirsty woman, and invited her to drink. I do not know whether the woman suspected some treachery, or whether she was merely frightened ; anyhow, she somewhat churlishly refused the kindly offer which had been made to her, and would not drink the buttermilk.

Naturally, the fairy was much offended. She summoned a number of other fairies to her aid, and they dragged the woman into the dun, and took her into a subterranean chamber. In this room was a great quantity of wool, a spinning wheel, and a girnal full of meal. The fairy said to the woman, " You see the wool, the spinning wheel, and the meal? You will remain a prisoner here till you have spun all the wool, and eaten all the meal. When you have done this, you will be set free, but not before." The woman was then left to set about the tasks which she had to accomplish.

For days she ate all the meal she could, and spun wool unceasingly, but neither the meal nor the wool seemed to decrease in quantity. The more wool she spun, the more there was to spin; the more she ate, the fuller the girnal seemed to grow. She began to fear that she was a prisoner in the Dun for life.

There was, however, another human being in the Dun, an old, old man, who had given some offence to the fairies years before, and who had grown grey in his captivity. He knew the pleasant little ways of the fairies, and he told the woman that, if she anointed her left eye with saliva before beginning her work, she would soon finish the meal and spin all the wool. She took the hint, and very soon the masses of wool and meal began to diminish, and, ere long, the woman's task was done.

The fairy had given her word, and fairies always keep their promises, so she had to set the woman at liberty, but, as she did so, she said savagely, " My curse be on the mouth that gave you the knowledge which enabled you to fulfil your task." The tale does not tell what she did to the old man.

A SECOND FAIRY TALE OF RHUAND HUNAN.

An old crone was lying fast asleep in her chair. Firmly clasped in her arms was a new-born babe. The mother was lying on a bed watching her infant. Her thoughts were sad. Three times a child of hers had been stolen by the fairies, and she could not forget her sorrows, but there, in the old woman's arms, was her consolation. She resolved that she would save this child from a similar fate at all costs.

But, as she lay and mused over the past, her heart sunk within her. Three tiny, hideous, wrinkled women appeared. The mother tried to leap up, tried to scream, but some magic spell kept her quiet. She watched the intruders with fear in her heart. They approached the chair where the sleeping nurse sat, and the oldest and ugliest of the three stretched out her arms to seize the child. One of her sisters, whose expression was kinder than that of the others, interfered. " Oh, spare this child," she said, " we have had three of her bairns ; may we not leave her this one ?" The old and ugly fairy turned savagely on her sister, and hissed out the words, " We will not take the babe, as you wish it, but the boon I grant is a small one." She pointed to the fireplace, and added, " When that brown peat on the hearth is burnt to grey ashes, the babe will die." Thus speaking, she left the room, followed by her sisters.

With their departure the spell which lay upon the mother was removed. She sprang to her feet, she seized the smouldering peat, she soaked it in water, and, wrapping it in a cloth, laid it in a chest where she kept her most precious possessions.

Years passed, the child grew up, and the mother had almost forgotten the visit of the fairies; but still she kept the peat safely locked up in her chest. The maiden was often curious as to what her mother so carefully guarded in this box, but she could never induce her to say anything about it.

When the girl was about 20, she was engaged to be married to a young neighbour, and the day of the wedding was drawing near. On the Sunday before the appointed day, the maiden did not accompany the rest of the family when they went to kirk. It is an old Highland custom that maidens should not appear at the kirk on the Sunday before their wedding day. She had nothing to do, and was wondering how she would put away the time till they all came back, when she noticed that her mother had accidentally left the carefully-guarded chest unlocked. She knew that she had no business to pry into her mother's secrets, but the curiosity of years was too strong for her, and she proceeded to turn out the contents of the chest.

At the very bottom was a linen cloth, carefully tied up with string. She cut the string, she opened the parcel, and found in it a half-burnt peat. She was lost in wonder at her mother so carefully preserving such a worthless thing. As she was examining the peat, it slipped from her fingers, and fell into the fire, which was burning on the open hearth in the middle of the room. She heard her relations returning, and, anxious to hide what she had been doing, she began to pack the things which she had taken out back into the chest. But, before she could finish, the peat had caught fire ; she felt a sudden pain at her heart, and fell fainting on the floor. Her parents came in ; she gasped out the tale of what she had done. The mother rushed to the fire, hoping even yet to save a fragment of the peat. Alas ! it was too late. ' The peat had become grey ash, and, as it did so, the maiden died. Thus the prophecy uttered by the wicked fairy twenty years before was fulfilled.

Fairies were not the only mythical beings in which the people firmly believed. Water kelpies were also to them extremely real.

The water kelpies, or water horses, were most hateful creatures. Their homes were in the lochs, whence they sallied forth to prey on human beings. They possessed the power of assuming the human form, but were often detected by their having much hair on their chests, and much sand in their hair. Strange as it seems, they possessed the gift of song in a remarkable degree. Beautiful singing was frequently heard on the lochs which they frequented, and mothers often used their songs to soothe a restless child,

A LEGEND OF GLEN BRITTLE.

A maiden, who lived at Glen Brittle, went one fine summer day to Tote-a-Bhain to bring home some peats. She reached the peat stack, filled her creel, and started on her homeward way. The day was hot, the creel was heavy, and, feeling tired, she sat down in the heather to rest.

While she was resting a stranger came by, a singularly attractive-looking young man. He stopped, entered into conversation with the girl, and presently sat down beside her. After a little talk, somewhat to his companion's surprise, he laid his head upon her knees, asked her to braid his hair, and, without waiting for an answer, fell asleep. As he did so, his shirt, which lacked a button, fell open, and she saw that on his chest was a mass of tangled hair. As she ran her fingers through his hair, she found that it was full of sand. She knew the signs, and she realised, with horror, that this pleasant looking youth was a water kelpie.

She gently laid his head on a tuft of heather, sprang to her feet, and fled. The kelpie woke, resumed his natural shape, and came after her in hot pursuit, uttering the most dreadful yells. Fear lent the maiden wings. She kept

ahead ; she reached her father's house, but, overcome with the
haste she had made, and with the awful terror which she felt,
she fell upon the threshold, dead.

A LEGEND OF BEN SGATH.

On Ben Sgath, a hill between Loch Bracadale and Loch
Snizort, stood in olden days a shieling. This gave shelter,
during a summer years ago, to eight maidens, who had come
up from Totarder to tend the cattle, and to make butter and
cheese. These maidens slept on a great bed of fragrant heather.
They were just about to lie down to rest one evening, when
an old woman came up, bent with age, and weary with travel.
She asked to be allowed to share their bed. The maidens at
once agreed, but, when the question arose as to where the
old woman should lie, they found that it was very difficult to
please her. They suggested that she should sleep at the foot
of the bed, at its head, at its sides, but none of these proposals
satisfied their guest. In each of these places, she said, a beast
would come and kill her in the night. She must lie in the
middle of the bed, with the girls on the outside of her. To
this at last they agreed. They all lay down, and all, excepting
two, were soon asleep.

By chance one of the maids, who was lying on the outside
of the bed, could not sleep that night. As she lay, restlessly
tossing from side to side, she heard sounds which convinced
her that the old woman was as wakeful as she was. In the
dim light of a Highland summer's night she saw enough to
show her what their guest was doing. She was sucking the
blood of the sleeping maidens. The old woman was a vampire,
a water kelpie in disguise.

The terrified maiden rose, silently slipped out of the hut,
and sought safety in flight. The kelpie saw her go, and,
casting off his disguise, followed her at tremendous speed.
Fast as the maiden went, and though a stern chase is a long
chase, the kelpie gained steadily. At last he was so near that
she could feel his hot breath on her neck. Though she was
now near her home at Totarder, she gave herself up for lost.

With one frantic, final effort she stumbled across a running burn, and, as she did so, she heard a cock crow in the hamlet below. She fell exhausted on the further side of the burn, and waited for her dreadful fate.

But, though she scarcely realised it, she was saved. A crowing cock affords a mysterious protection against evil spirits, and since no kelpie can cross running water, as she lay gasping in the heather, her dreaded foe stood beside the burn which had arrested his progress, saying in self-pity, " Duilich, duilich " (" Difficult " or " Hard " in Gaelic). The name of this burn is even now " Duilich." When the maiden had recovered a little, she made her way to her home, and told her father what had happened. He and some of his neighbours went up to the sheiling, and, on the great heather bed, they found the seven maidens lying dead. It is said that to this day, on the warmest summer day, a chill breeze blows across Ben Sgath, to remind us all of this dreadful tale.

TWO LEGENDS OF LOCH DUAGRICH.

Loch Duagrich, a broad sheet of water among the hills to the north-east of Loch Bracadale, was a favourite haunt of the water kelpies. Upon its shores a maiden, named Morag, met one day a young man, who found much favour in her eyes. They met again and again, the acquaintance ripened into love, and in due course the couple were married. Strange to say, they lived happily together for some months.

Then some accident broke the charm which disguised her husband, and she discovered that he was a kelpie. She got safely away from him, but the whole of her after life was over-shadowed by the thought that for months she had been the wife of a kelpie.

A young water kelpie, who lived with his parents in Loch Duagrich, did not come off so well in one of his adventures. Having assumed the appearance of a somewhat loutish-looking young man, he came one day to a cottage, and found the gude wife stirring porridge in a large pan. He asked the woman her name. This she did not feel inclined to give, so she answered, " Mifhein us mifhein " (" Myself and Myself.") He then asked her what she was doing, and she told him that she was making porridge. Meanwhile the woman was watching her guest closely. She saw how brown his chest was, and how full of sand was his hair, so she made up her mind that he was a kelpie.

Presently he asked her to give him some of the porridge which she was making. " Yes," she cried, " you shall have it all," and, so speaking, she seized the pot, and poured its boiling contents on his head. The heat broke the spell which had worked his disguise. He rushed from the cottage roaring with pain. He told his parents that he had been most frightfully scalded. They asked him who had injured him. " Mifhein us mifhein has done it," he answered. " Oh, well," said his father, " if you have done it yourself we cannot do anything to punish your enemy." Thus the woman suffered no harm, but she was ever afterwards very suspicious of any strangers who chanced to enter her cottage.

A LEGEND OF BEN FROCHDAIDH.

A farmer who lived beneath the shadow of Ben Frochdaidh, a hill between Talisker and Drynoch, once mortally offended a kelpie, whose home was in a loch in Glendale. Determined to be revenged, the kelpie, in the form and dress of a serving man, sought out the farmer, and asked for employment. This the farmer, suspecting no evil, gave him, and the disguised kelpie served him faithfully and well for seven years. But all the time he was waiting for his opportunity, and, when at last it came, he ruthlessly killed his master, and returned to his loch in Glendale.

Yet another mysterious person in whom the people believed, was the gruagach. He was a handsome lad, with golden hair and a white chest, which was generally bare. He was to be found in byres and sheilings, and wherever the cattle were. He had the greatest love for them, and would punish any injury done to them with the rod which he always carried. The merest touch of this rod was sufficient to cause death.

A LEGEND OF GLEN MACCASKILL.

In the olden times a woman and her daughter were living in a sheiling, which stood in Glen MacCaskill. One night they heard that the cattle were very disturbed and rest-less, and the daughter went out to see what was the matter. She could discover no cause, but there was no doubt that, for some hidden reason, all the cattle were perturbed about something. One cow especially seemed to be possessed with an evil spirit. The girl lost her temper, and swore at the cow.

Then she discovered the cause of the trouble—the grua-gach was there. Though it was all his own fault, he was furious at the words the maiden had spoken to the cow. He struck her with his rod, and she fell dead at his feet.

The mother saw her daughter fall. It was some time before she realised that the girl was dead, but, when she did, she flung herself down beside her child, and spent the whole night in bitter lamentations.

The gruagach was filled with remorse. Till daylight came he stood beside the door, grasping the lintel beam in his hand, and gazing down on the sad scene before him, on his victim's body and on her mourning mother. He then slowly and sadly departed, and went no man knew where.

MERMAIDS.

The sea had its mysterious beings as well as the mountains and fresh-water lochs. One old man used to tell how his grandfather had once found a young mermaid, about ten or twelve years old, entangled in his long lines when he took them up one morning. It resembled a human being as far as the waist, but below that it was like a fish. The poor thing was dead when it was brought to the surface, and the fisherman left it on the shore. To his surprise, even after it had lain there for some time, it remained quite fresh, and finally he took it out to sea in his boat, and consigned the poor dead mermaid to her native element in the Minch.

Even in recent times mermaids have been occasionally seen. Not very long ago some boys went down one Sunday morning to bathe in Loch Dunvegan. As they were taking off their clothes previous to entering the water, they saw someone swimming towards them with extraordinary grace and skill.

At first they thought that it was a boy from a neighbouring township, but, when she came nearer, they saw that it was a very beautiful mermaid. They watched her till she swam away out of sight, and, being thoroughly frightened, resolved that they would never again break the Sabbath by bathing upon the holy day.

The following story indicates that the universal belief in witchcraft was shared by the West Highlands :—

A LEGEND OF ULLINISH.

The gude man of Ullinish, as he thought, was happily married. He had lived for years with his wife, and never suspected that all the time she was a witch, and was practising the black art in secret. At last his eyes were opened to the terrible truth. One day his serving man came to him, and gave him notice that he wished to leave his service. The farmer asked him his reason, saying that he did not think that he had been a bad master. "Oh, no," said the man, "it is not the gude man I am complaining of, but the gude wife. You do not know it, but I know it too well. She is a witch, and every night she comes out, she speaks some spell, and turns me into a horse. Then she rides me all over the country; sometimes she has ridden me to places in France. I cannot stand it any longer. That is my reason for wishing to leave."

The gude man of Ullinish was horrified, and did not know what to do. At last a thought occurred to him. One of the "wise men," who were always to be found in the Highlands, lived in the neighbourhood, and the best plan was to go and tell him. So master and man went off together to consult the wise man. He was quite equal to the occasion, and told the serving man what to do. "When next she comes out," he said, "be ready with a bridle and bit in your hands, as she speaks her spell, throw the bridle over her head, and she will become a mare; her spell will recoil on herself."

That very night the gude wife came out; the serving man implicitly obeyed the sage's directions, and the witch was turned into a mare. They took her to a smith, and, by their directions, he placed iron horse-shoes on her hind feet. The

next morning the gude wife was very ill, and died in the after-
noon. When they laid out her body for burial, horse-shoes
were found on her feet. This conclusively proved the truth
of the story.

Two other superstitions are dealt with in the following
stories :—

PUTTING DEATH PAST ONESELF.

A man named Donald MacQueen was fishing one day
with a companion, when he heard a voice calling him—
"Donald MacQueen, Donald MacQueen." He immediately
cried out, "It is no me you are meaning; it's Donald MacQueen
of Ose."

Some days afterwards they came home, and, as they
neared the shore in Loch Bracadale, they saw a funeral procession leaving the house at Ose. Donald's companion said
to him, "Donald, you have killed that man." "Maybe I
have," said Donald, "but a man will do a great deal to put
death past himself."

This story illustrates a superstition that if a man hears
his name called at sea, it means that he is going to die, but
that, if he can think of a namesake, and shout, as Donald
MacQueen did, that it is not himself who is meant, he will put
death past himself, and his namesake will die.

THE BLEEDING BONE—A LEGEND OF DRYNOCH.

The following story is a curious variant of the well-known
belief that the wounds of a murdered man will break out
bleeding afresh on the approach of his murderer.

The tenant of Drynoch moved a shepherd, named Mac-
Millan, who had previously lived at Meidle, to Drynoch, and
repaired an old ruined cottage for his reception. One fine
winter night, soon after MacMillan had taken up his quarters
in the old cottage, he and his wife were disturbed by someone knocking at the door. MacMillan got up, went to the
door, and found that an old man was there, who wanted
shelter for the night. He willingly acceded to the old man's
request. Mrs MacMillan got up, supplied the old fellow with

something to eat, told him that he could sleep on some heather, which she piled up in the corner of the living room, and gave him a plaid to keep him warm. The old man lay down on the shake-down which they had prepared for him, and MacMillan and his wife went back to bed.

But they were not long undisturbed. The old man kept complaining that "wet soot" was falling on him from the wall beneath which he was lying. MacMillan got up again, and lighted a candle. He found that there was really something pouring down the wall, but it was not wet soot; it was blood.

The terrified old man then made a dreadful confession. Years before he had quarrelled with a neighbour here at Drynoch; he had killed his adversary, and concealed the body in the wall of an old ruined cottage, piling up some stones to conceal the evidence of his guilt. He had fled the country, and been a wanderer on the face of the earth for a long time. Now he had been impelled, by some strange, irresistible impulse, to re-visit the scene of his crime. "Now let me go," he said, and stumbled out into the darkness, and was never seen again.

The next morning MacMillan told his master what had happened. They examined the cottage, and, in the wall, they found the bones of the murdered man. From these bones had poured the stream of blood which had terrified the murderer.

THE END.

INDEX

INDEX

A

R

S

T

U

V

W